Revise 11+

Also available to support
Non-Verbal Reasoning 11+ revision:

Non-Verbal Reasoning
Practice Book 2

Series Consultant: Harry Smith
Author: Gareth Moore

THE REVISE 11+ SERIES

For the full range of Pearson Revise 11+ titles visit:
www.pearsonschools.co.uk/revise11plus

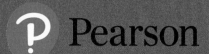

Contents

How to use this book

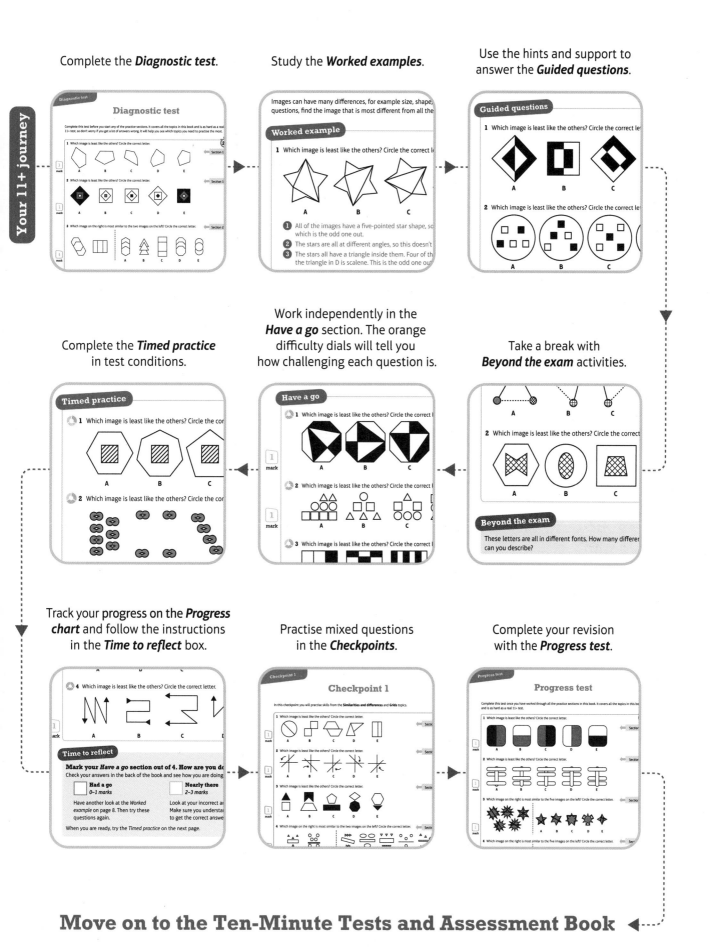

Complete the *Diagnostic test*.

Study the *Worked examples*.

Use the hints and support to answer the *Guided questions*.

Complete the *Timed practice* in test conditions.

Work independently in the *Have a go* section. The orange difficulty dials will tell you how challenging each question is.

Take a break with *Beyond the exam* activities.

Track your progress on the *Progress chart* and follow the instructions in the *Time to reflect* box.

Practise mixed questions in the *Checkpoints*.

Complete your revision with the *Progress test*.

Move on to the Ten-Minute Tests and Assessment Book

Diagnostic test

Complete this test before you start any of the practice sections. It covers all the topics in this book and is as hard as a real 11+ test, so don't worry if you get a lot of answers wrong. It will help you see which topics you need to practise the most.

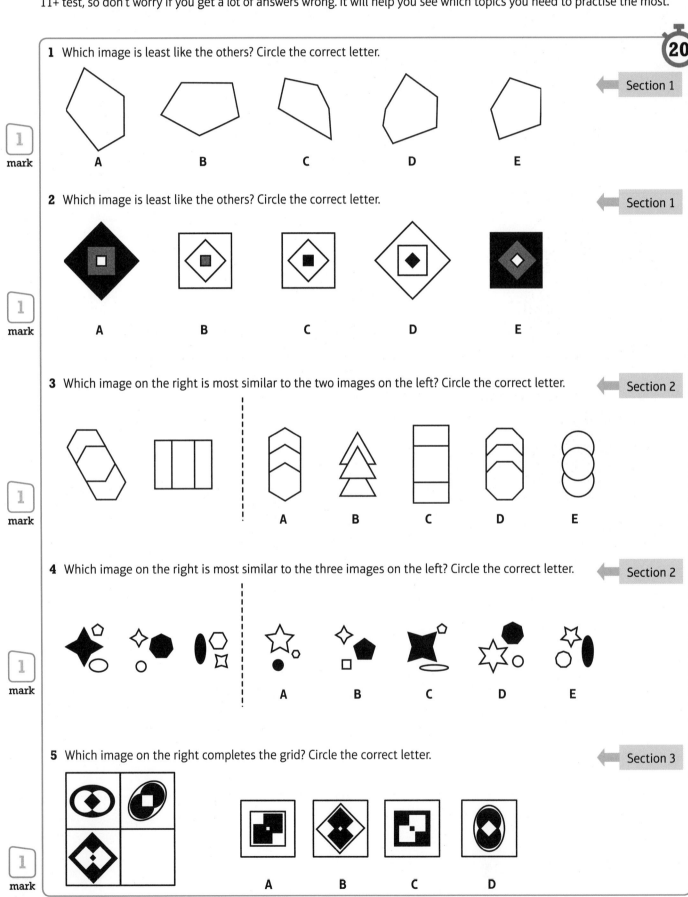

20

1 Which image is least like the others? Circle the correct letter.

Section 1

A   B   C   D   E

1 mark

2 Which image is least like the others? Circle the correct letter.

Section 1

A   B   C   D   E

1 mark

3 Which image on the right is most similar to the two images on the left? Circle the correct letter.

Section 2

A   B   C   D   E

1 mark

4 Which image on the right is most similar to the three images on the left? Circle the correct letter.

Section 2

A   B   C   D   E

1 mark

5 Which image on the right completes the grid? Circle the correct letter.

Section 3

A   B   C   D

1 mark

6 Which image on the right completes the grid? Circle the correct letter.

Section 3

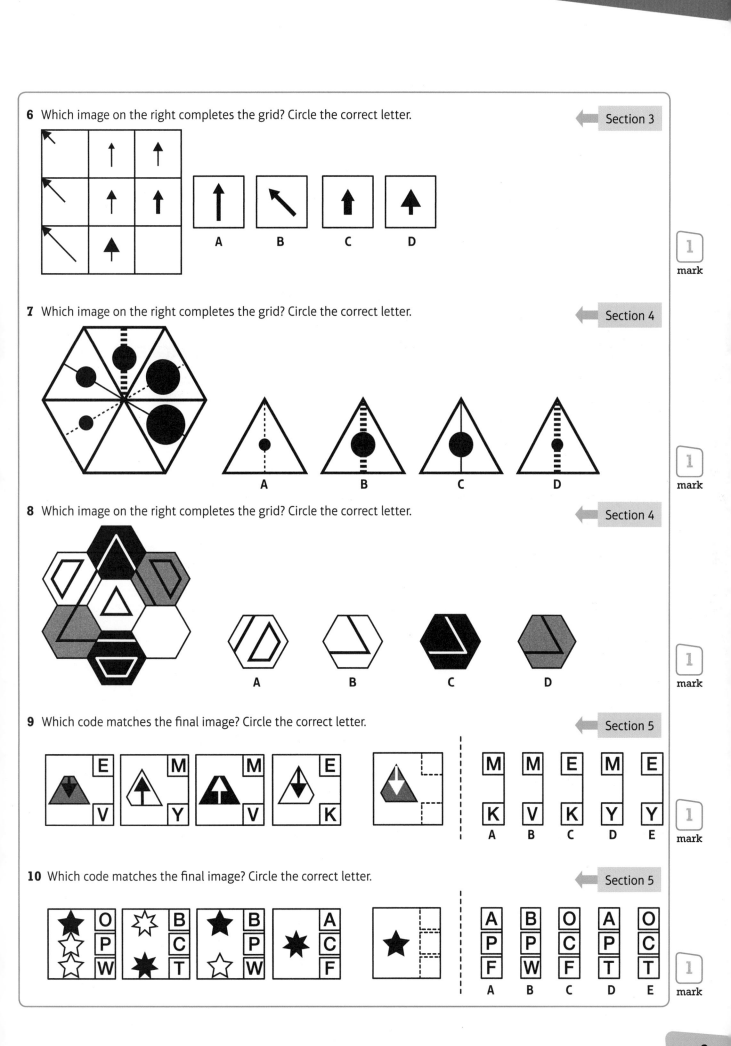

A   B   C   D

1 mark

7 Which image on the right completes the grid? Circle the correct letter.

Section 4

A   B   C   D

1 mark

8 Which image on the right completes the grid? Circle the correct letter.

Section 4

A   B   C   D

1 mark

9 Which code matches the final image? Circle the correct letter.

Section 5

A   B   C   D   E

1 mark

10 Which code matches the final image? Circle the correct letter.

Section 5

A   B   C   D   E

1 mark

11 Which code matches the final image? Circle the correct letter.

Section 6

1 mark

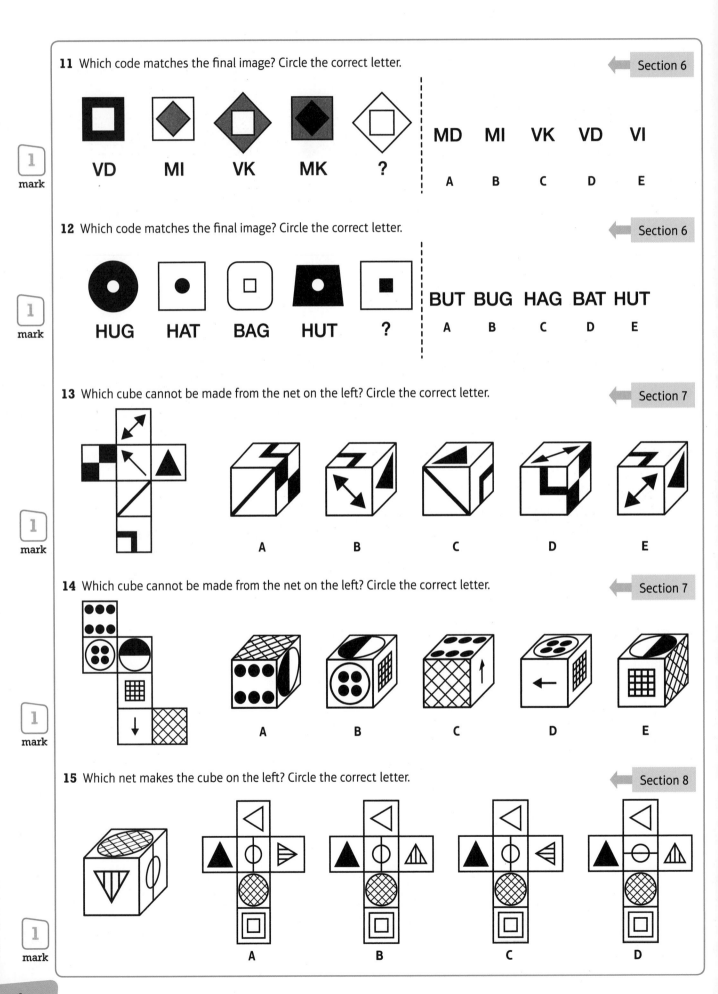

VD   MI   VK   MK   ?

MD	MI	VK	VD	VI
A	B	C	D	E

12 Which code matches the final image? Circle the correct letter.

Section 6

1 mark

HUG   HAT   BAG   HUT   ?

BUT	BUG	HAG	BAT	HUT
A	B	C	D	E

13 Which cube cannot be made from the net on the left? Circle the correct letter.

Section 7

1 mark

A   B   C   D   E

14 Which cube cannot be made from the net on the left? Circle the correct letter.

Section 7

1 mark

A   B   C   D   E

15 Which net makes the cube on the left? Circle the correct letter.

Section 8

1 mark

A   B   C   D

4

16 Which net makes the cube on the left? Circle the correct letter.

Section 8

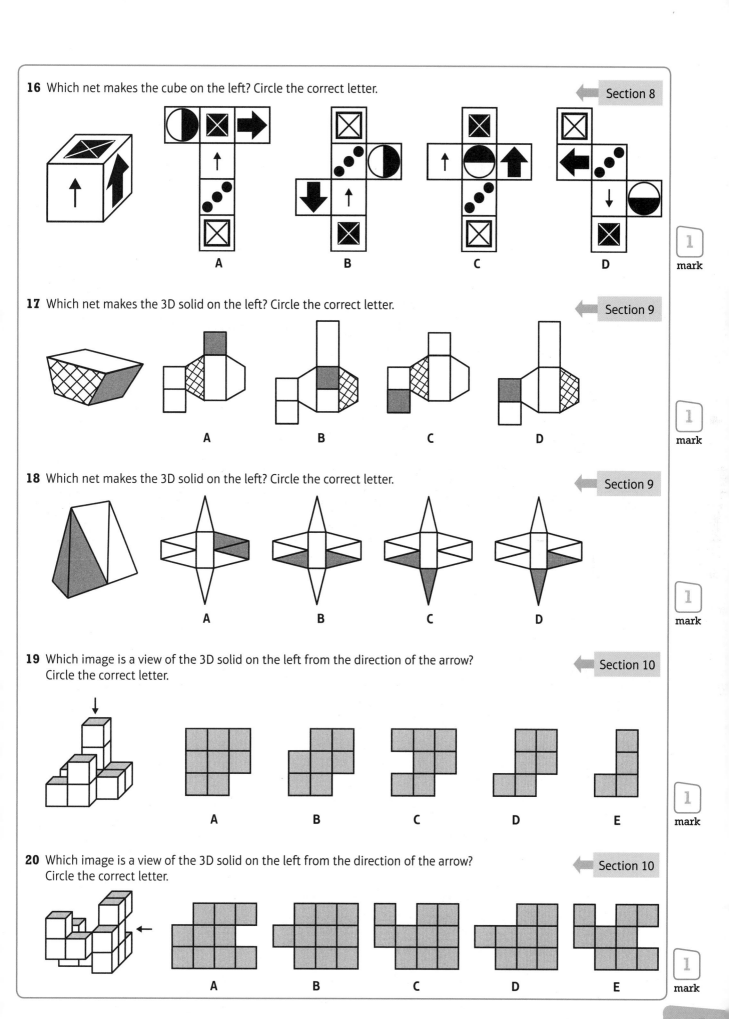

A   **B**   **C**   **D**

1 mark

17 Which net makes the 3D solid on the left? Circle the correct letter.

Section 9

A   **B**   **C**   **D**

1 mark

18 Which net makes the 3D solid on the left? Circle the correct letter.

Section 9

A   **B**   **C**   **D**

1 mark

19 Which image is a view of the 3D solid on the left from the direction of the arrow? Circle the correct letter.

Section 10

A   **B**   **C**   **D**   **E**

1 mark

20 Which image is a view of the 3D solid on the left from the direction of the arrow? Circle the correct letter.

Section 10

A   **B**   **C**   **D**   **E**

1 mark

Look at these 3D solids.

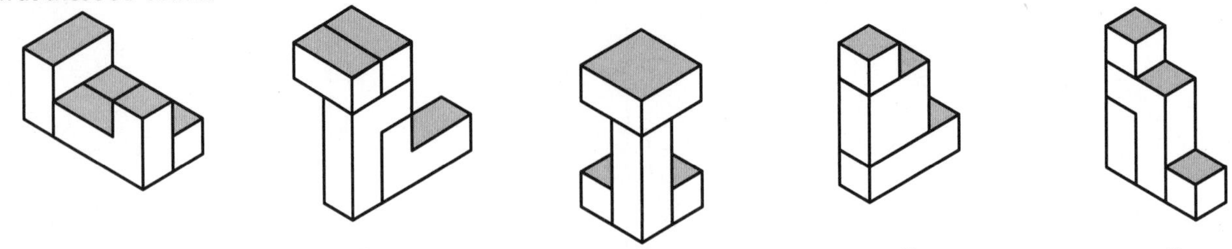

A   B   C   D   E

21 Which of the 3D solids at the top of the page has been rotated to make this view? Circle the correct letter.   Section 11

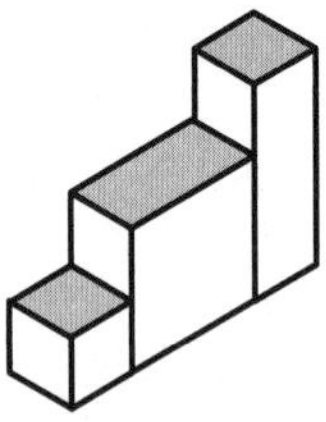

A   B   C   D   E

1 mark

22 Which of the 3D solids at the top of the page has been rotated to make this view? Circle the correct letter.   Section 11

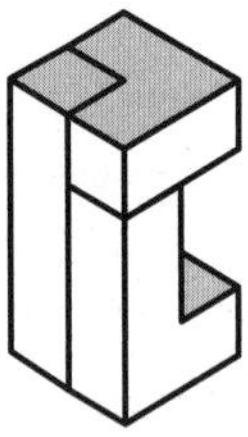

A   B   C   D   E

1 mark

23 Which view shows the 3D solid on the left from the direction of the arrow? Circle the correct letter.   Section 12

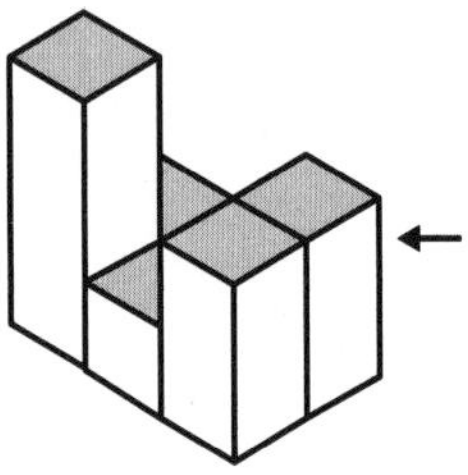

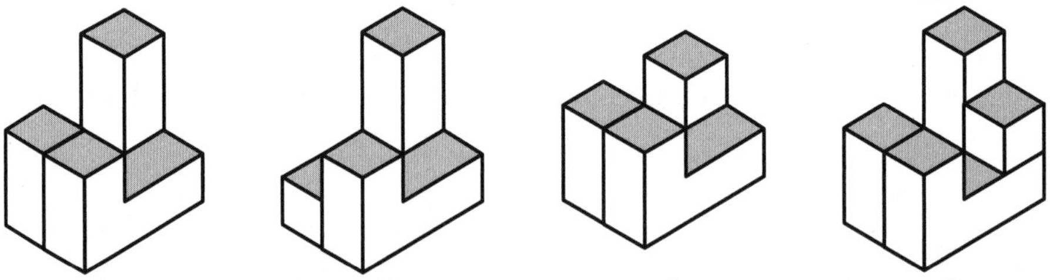

A   B   C   D

1 mark

24 Which view shows the 3D solid on the left from the direction of the arrow? Circle the correct letter.   Section 12

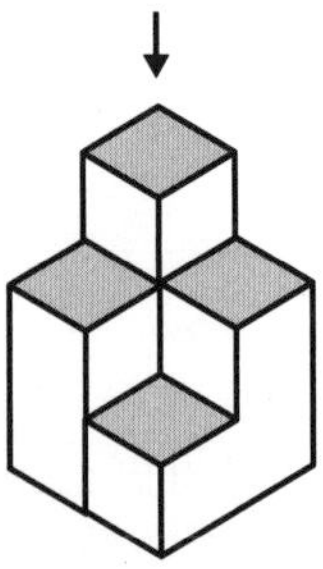

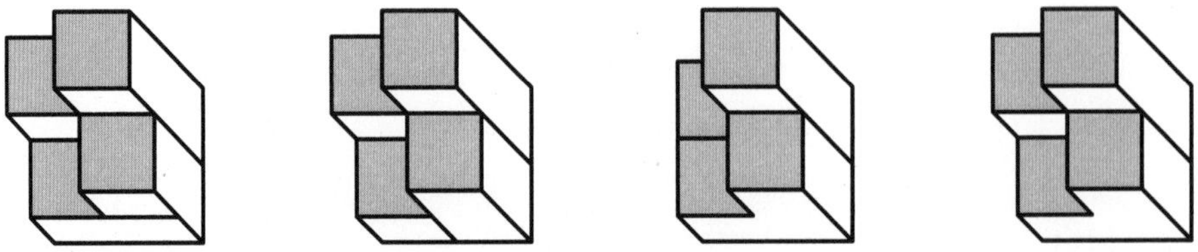

A   B   C   D

1 mark

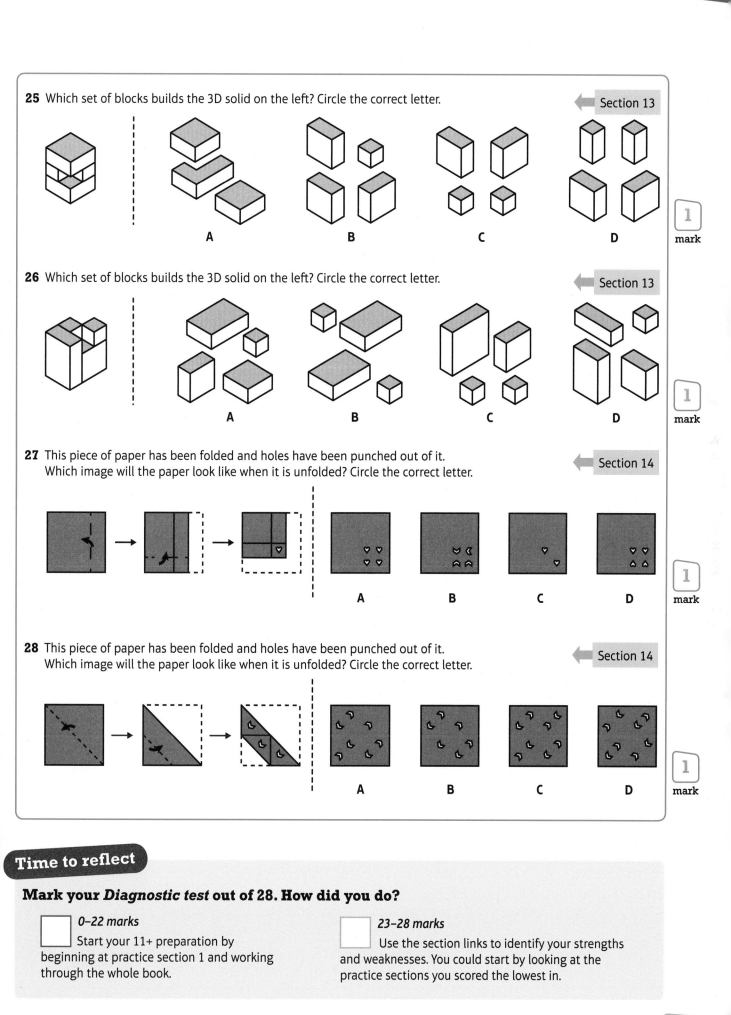

25 Which set of blocks builds the 3D solid on the left? Circle the correct letter.

Section 13

A   B   C   D

1 mark

26 Which set of blocks builds the 3D solid on the left? Circle the correct letter.

Section 13

A   B   C   D

1 mark

27 This piece of paper has been folded and holes have been punched out of it.
Which image will the paper look like when it is unfolded? Circle the correct letter.

Section 14

A   B   C   D

1 mark

28 This piece of paper has been folded and holes have been punched out of it.
Which image will the paper look like when it is unfolded? Circle the correct letter.

Section 14

A   B   C   D

1 mark

Time to reflect

Mark your *Diagnostic test* out of 28. How did you do?

0–22 marks
Start your 11+ preparation by beginning at practice section 1 and working through the whole book.

23–28 marks
Use the section links to identify your strengths and weaknesses. You could start by looking at the practice sections you scored the lowest in.

1 Odd one out

Images can have many differences, for example size, shape, number of parts, colour, rotation or reflection. In each of these questions, find the image that is most different from all the others.

Worked example

1 Which image is least like the others? Circle the correct letter.

A   B   C   (D)   E

One of these images is different from the others in some way. Find something that is the same in all but one of the images.

1 All of the images have a five-pointed star shape, so the shape doesn't tell you which is the odd one out.

2 The stars are all at different angles, so this doesn't tell you the odd one out.

3 The stars all have a triangle inside them. Four of the triangles are isosceles, but the triangle in D is scalene. This is the odd one out.

123 An isosceles triangle has two sides that are the same length. A scalene triangle has sides that are all different lengths.

Guided questions

1 Which image is least like the others? Circle the correct letter.

   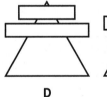 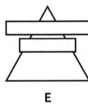

A   B   C   D   E

Each image contains the same three shapes, arranged in a different way. Look at how they are arranged to find the odd one out.

1 In B, D and E, the rectangles are close together. In A, the rectangles are further apart. But they are further apart in C too, so this doesn't mean A is the odd one out.

2 In D and E, the rectangles are at the top of the triangle. In B, the rectangles are in the middle. In A and C, there is one rectangle at the bottom and one at the top.

3 In A, B, C and D, the smaller rectangle is on top. E is the only image with the bigger rectangle on top.

2 Which image is least like the others? Circle the correct letter.

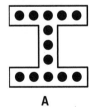 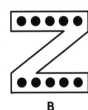 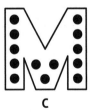 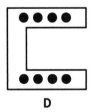 

A   B   C   D   E

Although these images look like letters, you need to think of them as shapes.

1 Count the number of sides each shape has.

2 Count the number of dots in each shape.

3 Find a link between the number of sides and the number of dots.

Guided questions

1 Which image is least like the others? Circle the correct letter.

A   B   C   D   E

> Each image contains two black sections and two white sections. Focus on the inner shapes in each image and then on the outer shapes in each image.

2 Which image is least like the others? Circle the correct letter.

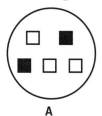 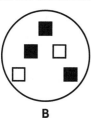 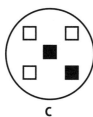 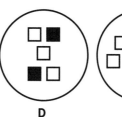 

A   B   C   D   E

> Each circle contains five black and white squares. Try looking at how the squares are arranged, the pattern of the colours and how many of each colour there are.

Have a go

1 Which image is least like the others? Circle the correct letter.

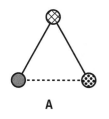 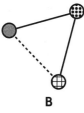 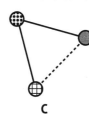 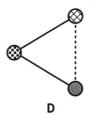 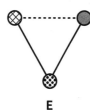

A   B   C   D   E

> Look at the shading of the shapes and the style of the lines. Work out what is different in each image.

 mark

2 Which image is least like the others? Circle the correct letter.

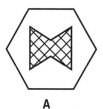 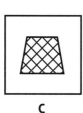 

A   B   C   D   E

> If the shapes are all different, look for something else that they might have in common. Try looking at the number of sides each shape has.

 mark

Beyond the exam

These letters are all in different fonts. How many differences between the letters can you describe?

Have a go

1 Which image is least like the others? Circle the correct letter.

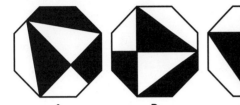

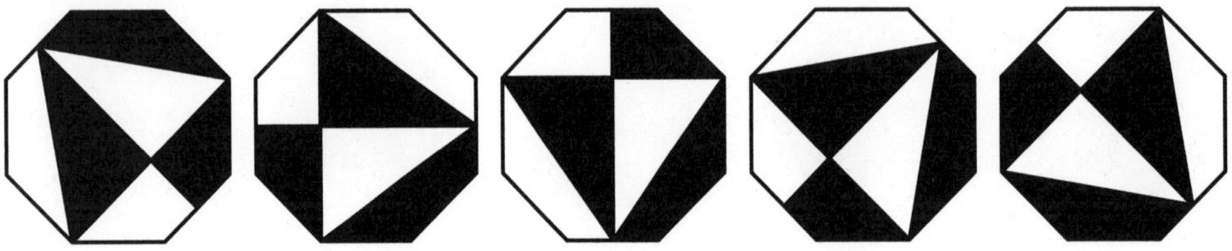

1 mark

If the images are very similar, try thinking about rotations and reflections.

A   B   C   D   E

2 Which image is least like the others? Circle the correct letter.

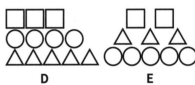

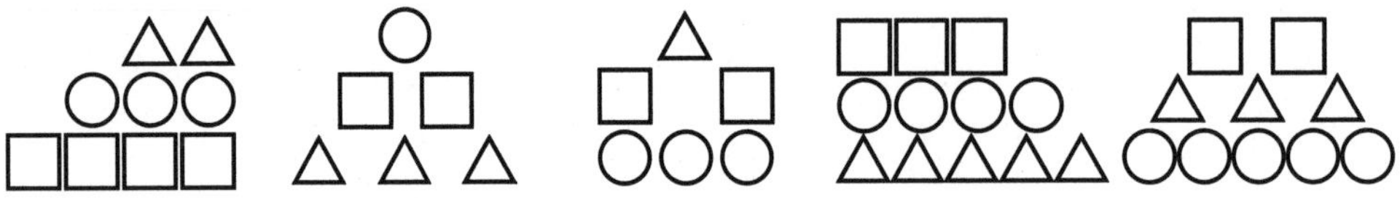

1 mark

If the images contain lots of different shapes, look at size, shape, number and how the shapes are arranged.

A   B   C   D   E

3 Which image is least like the others? Circle the correct letter.

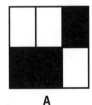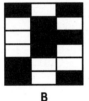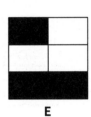

1 mark

If the images are made up of lots of smaller shapes, try counting how many smaller shapes make up each image.

A   B   C   D   E

4 Which image is least like the others? Circle the correct letter.

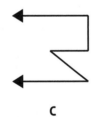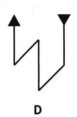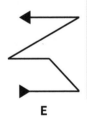

1 mark

Several things might change in each image. See if you can find something that stays the same.

A   B   C   D   E

Time to reflect

Mark your *Have a go* section out of 4. How are you doing so far?

Check your answers in the back of the book and see how you are doing.

Had a go 0–1 marks	**Nearly there** 2–3 marks	**Nailed it!** 4 marks
Have another look at the *Worked example* on page 8. Then try these questions again.	Look at your incorrect answers. Make sure you understand how to get the correct answer.	Congratulations! Now see whether you can get full marks on the *Timed practice*.

When you are ready, try the *Timed practice* on the next page.

Timed practice

4

1 Which image is least like the others? Circle the correct letter.

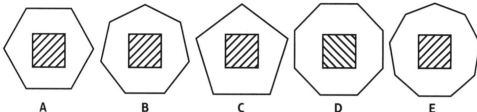

   A   B   C   D   E

| 1 |
| mark |

2 Which image is least like the others? Circle the correct letter.

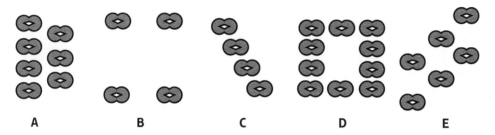

   A   B   C   D   E

| 1 |
| mark |

3 Which image is least like the others? Circle the correct letter.

   A   B   C   D   E

| 1 |
| mark |

4 Which image is least like the others? Circle the correct letter.

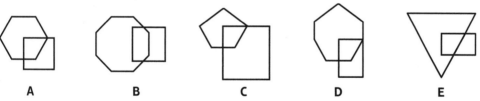

   A   B   C   D   E

| 1 |
| mark |

5 Which image is least like the others? Circle the correct letter.

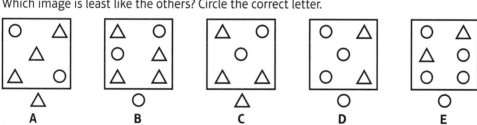

   A   B   C   D   E

| 1 |
| mark |

Time to reflect

Mark your *Timed practice* section out of 5. How did you do?
Check your answers in the back of the book and write your score in the progress chart.

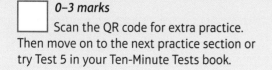
0–3 marks
Scan the QR code for extra practice.
Then move on to the next practice section or
try Test 5 in your Ten-Minute Tests book.

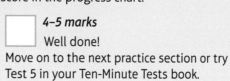
4–5 marks
Well done!
Move on to the next practice section or try
Test 5 in your Ten-Minute Tests book.

2 Which image belongs?

In each of these questions, find which image on the right belongs with the images on the left. All the images are similar in some way, but you need to find the image that is most similar.

Worked example

1 Which image on the right is most similar to the five images on the left? Circle the correct letter.

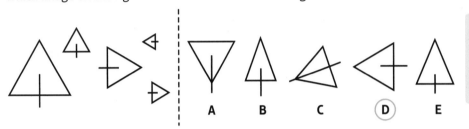

Find features that the images on the left share. Then decide which image on the right shares the most similarities with them.

1 The triangles on the left have a line going through a side, but not through a vertex. In A and C, the line goes through a vertex of the triangle, so they do not belong.

123 An equilateral triangle has sides that are all the same length.

2 The triangles on the left are different sizes and point in different directions, so you do not need to look for these features.

3 The triangles on the left are all equilaterals. In B and E, the triangle is not equilateral, so you can cross these options out. This means that D must be the right answer.

Guided questions

1 Which image on the right is most similar to the three images on the left? Circle the correct letter.

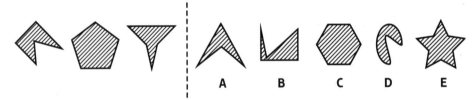

Try making a list of the features that the images on the left share.

1 All the shapes have the same shading, so this won't help you find the correct answer.

2 The shapes on the left are different sizes and have sides of different lengths, so this won't help you find the correct answer.

3 Count the number of sides that the shapes on the left have. Compare this with the images on the right.

2 Which image on the right is most similar to the five images on the left? Circle the correct letter.

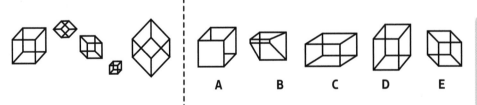

123 Remember that the faces of a cube are all squares. This means that all of a cube's edges must be the same length.

1 The images on the left are all cubes.

2 The cubes on the left all have transparent faces.

3 Look for the image on the right that shares these features.

Beyond the exam

Think of pairs of very different objects or animals. Can you describe something similar about them? For example, an elephant and a tractor are both heavy.

Guided questions

1 Which image on the right is most similar to the two images on the left?
Circle the correct letter.

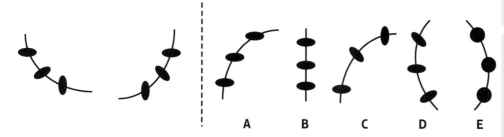

A   B   C   D   E

> Each of the images on the left contains three ovals and a curved line.
>
> Look at how the ovals overlap the line and which direction they point in. Think about whether they are vertical, horizontal or diagonal.

2 Which image on the right is most similar to the three images on the left?
Circle the correct letter.

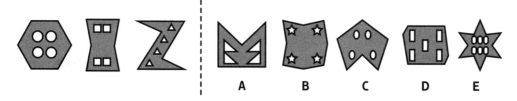

A   B   C   D   E

> The shapes in these images are all different. Think about the number of sides each shape has instead.

> Look at the number of small shapes that are in each bigger shape and where they are placed. Work out what they have in common.

Have a go

1 Which image on the right is most similar to the five images on the left?
Circle the correct letter.

> Think about the number of parts each image has.

A   B   C   D   E

1 mark

2 Which image on the right is most similar to the four images on the left?
Circle the correct letter.

A   B   C   D   E

> Look for different types of similarity one by one, such as how many times the shapes are repeated, how they are positioned, and the style of the lines and shading.

1 mark

Have a go

1 Which image on the right is most similar to the three images on the left? Circle the correct letter.

1 mark

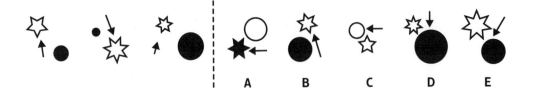

A   B   C   D   E

If the images have arrows, think about the direction they point in.

2 Which image on the right is most similar to the two images on the left? Circle the correct letter.

1 mark

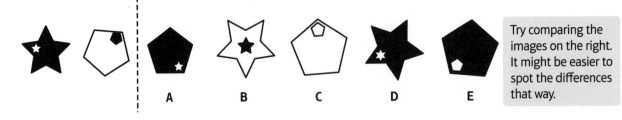

A   B   C   D   E

Try comparing the images on the right. It might be easier to spot the differences that way.

3 Which image on the right is most similar to the three images on the left? Circle the correct letter.

1 mark

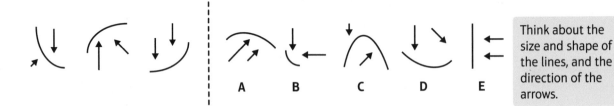

A   B   C   D   E

Think about the size and shape of the lines, and the direction of the arrows.

4 Which image on the right is most similar to the four images on the left? Circle the correct letter.

1 mark

A   B   C   D   E

If an image is made up of lots of shapes, look for repeated shapes.

Time to reflect

Mark your *Have a go* section out of 4. How are you doing so far?

Check your answers in the back of the book and see how you are doing.

Had a go	**Nearly there**	**Nailed it!**
0–1 marks	*2–3 marks*	*4 marks*
Have another look at the *Worked example* on page 12. Then try these questions again.	Look at your incorrect answers. Make sure you understand how to get the correct answer.	Congratulations! Now see whether you can get full marks on the *Timed practice*.

When you are ready, try the *Timed practice* on the next page.

Timed practice

1 Which image on the right is most similar to the five images on the left? Circle the correct letter.

A   B   C   D   E

1 mark

2 Which image on the right is most similar to the five images on the left? Circle the correct letter.

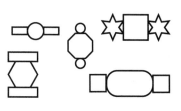 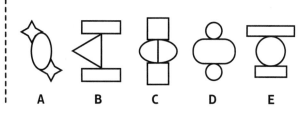

A   B   C   D   E

1 mark

3 Which image on the right is most similar to the three images on the left? Circle the correct letter.

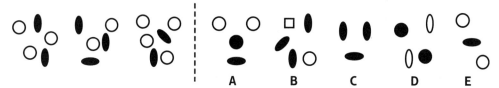

A   B   C   D   E

1 mark

4 Which image on the right is most similar to the three images on the left? Circle the correct letter.

 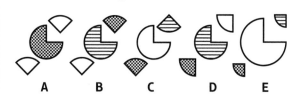

A   B   C   D   E

1 mark

5 Which image on the right is most similar to the four images on the left? Circle the correct letter.

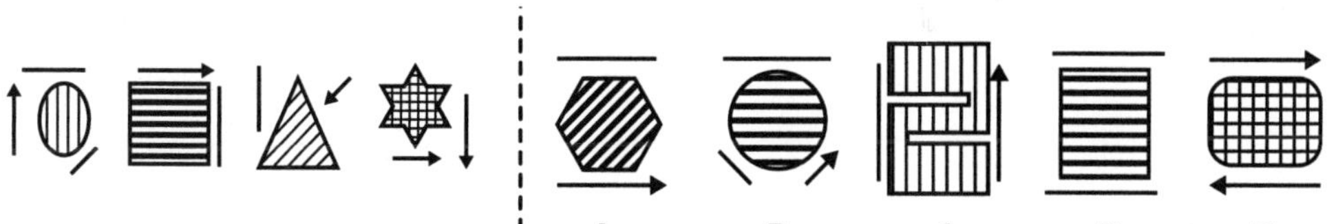

A   B   C   D   E

1 mark

Time to reflect

Mark your *Timed practice* section out of 5. How did you do?
Check your answers in the back of the book and write your score in the progress chart.

☐ *0–3 marks*
Scan the QR code for extra practice.
Then move on to the next practice section or
try Test 7 in your Ten-Minute Tests book.

☐ *4–5 marks*
Well done!
Move on to the next practice section or try
Test 7 in your Ten-Minute Tests book.

3 Complete the square grid

Each of these questions shows a grid with an empty square. Find which image on the right completes the pattern or sequence in the grid.

1 Which image on the right completes the grid? Circle the correct letter.

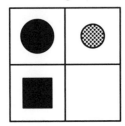

    A   B   Ⓒ   D

> Look for patterns in size, colour, shape, line style, rotation and reflection.

1 Reading across the first row, the large black circle on the left becomes a smaller, dotted circle on the right. Reading across the second row, the large black square on the left should become a smaller, dotted square on the right.

2 You can also read the grid down the columns. The big black circle at the top becomes a big black square at the bottom, so the small dotted circle at the top should become a small dotted square at the bottom.

1 Which image on the right completes the grid? Circle the correct letter.

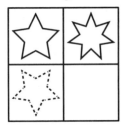

    A   B   C   D

> Read across the rows and down the columns of the grid to spot the pattern.

1 Reading across, the number of points on the star increases from five to seven.

2 Reading down, the star is reflected vertically and its outline changes from solid to dashed.

3 Use these rules to decide which image should appear in the empty square.

2 Which image on the right completes the grid? Circle the correct letter.

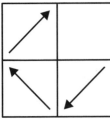

    A   B   C   D

> In this question, decide which image should go in the top-right square of the grid.

1 Instead of reading across the rows and down the columns, try looking at the whole pattern in the grid.

2 The arrows form three sides of a square. Each arrow points at the next one. Going around the grid clockwise, the arrow is rotated 90° each time.

Use the square grid template on page 97 to make your own grid question. Challenge a friend to find the correct answer.

Guided questions

1 Which image on the right completes the grid? Circle the correct letter.

This grid has three rows and three columns. Use the same steps as before to find the answer.

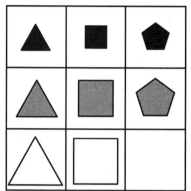

      A   **B**   **C**   **D**

1 Each row contains the same three shapes in the same order from left to right.

2 In each column, the shape gets larger from top to bottom.

3 The shapes are black in the first row, grey in the second row and white in the third row.

2 Which image on the right completes the grid? Circle the correct letter.

You might need to read diagonally, instead of across and down, to find a pattern.

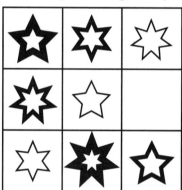

      A   **B**   **C**   **D**

1 Reading diagonally from top left to bottom right, the number of points on the stars stays the same but the line thickness changes.

2 Looking diagonally top right to bottom left, the line thickness stays the same but the number of points on the stars changes.

Have a go

1 Which image on the right completes the grid? Circle the correct letter.

You can't rotate the images before they go into the grid.

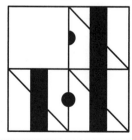

      A   **B**   **C**   **D**

1 mark

Have a go

1 Which image on the right completes the grid? Circle the correct letter.

In some questions you need to find the correct image to complete a shape or pattern.

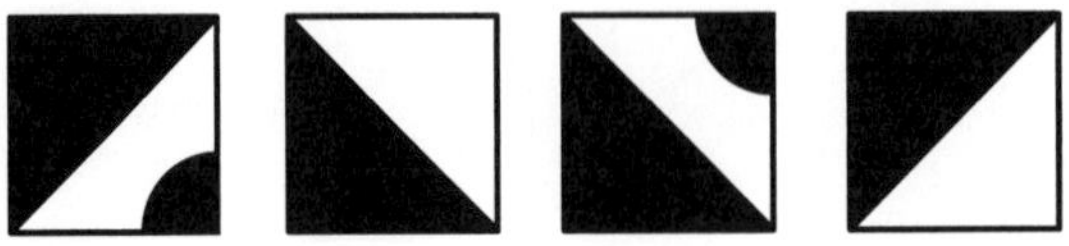

A   B   C   D

1 mark

2 Which image on the right completes the grid? Circle the correct letter.

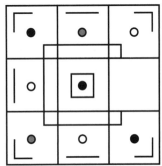

A grid might have two patterns at once. For example, you might need to complete a shape, as well as looking for a sequence.

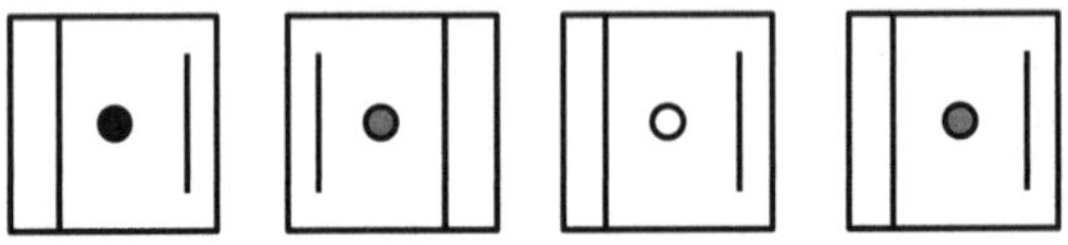

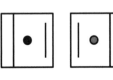

A   B   C   D

1 mark

3 Which image on the right completes the grid? Circle the correct letter.

If there are lots of shapes in the grid, try looking at each one separately.

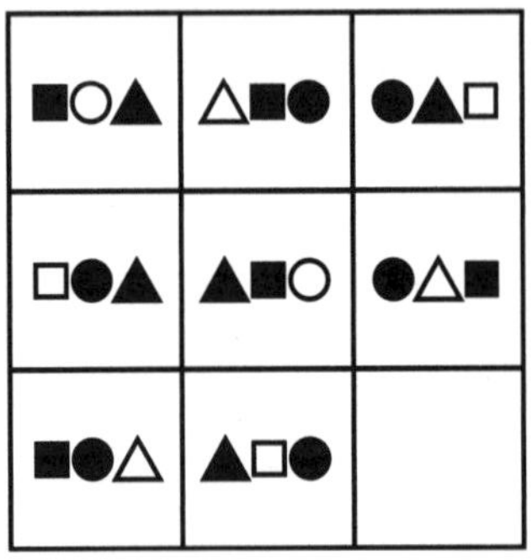

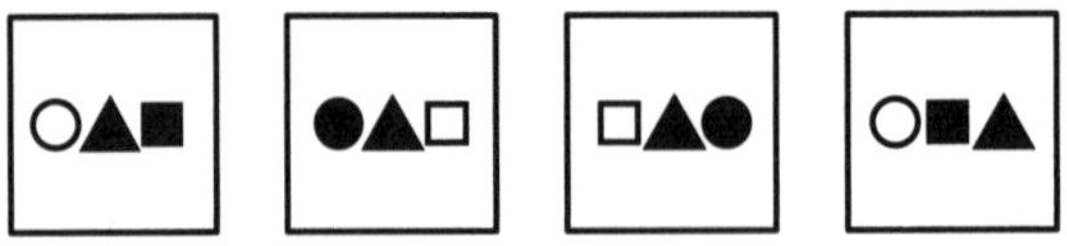

■○▲	△■●	●▲□
□●▲	▲■○	●△■
■●△	▲□●	

○▲■	●▲□	□▲●	○■▲
A	B	C	D

1 mark

Time to reflect

Mark your *Have a go* section out of 3. How are you doing so far?

Check your answers in the back of the book and see how you are doing.

| **Had a go** 0–1 marks | **Nearly there** 2 marks | **Nailed it!** 3 marks |

Have another look at the *Worked example* on page 16. Then try these questions again.

Look at your incorrect answers. Make sure you understand how to get the correct answer.

Congratulations! Now see whether you can get full marks on the *Timed practice*.

When you are ready, try the *Timed practice* on the next page.

Timed practice

1 Which image on the right completes the grid? Circle the correct letter.

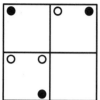 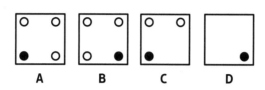

A   B   C   D

1 mark

2 Which image on the right completes the grid? Circle the correct letter.

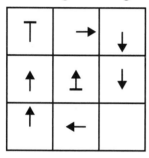 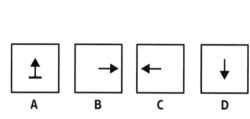

A   B   C   D

1 mark

3 Which image on the right completes the grid? Circle the correct letter.

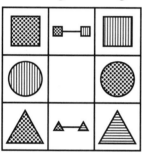 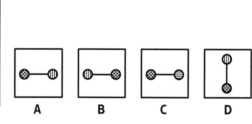

A   B   C   D

1 mark

4 Which image on the right completes the grid? Circle the correct letter.

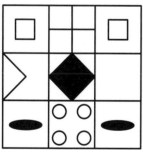 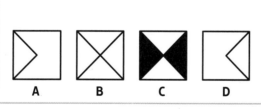

A   B   C   D

1 mark

Time to reflect

Mark your *Timed practice* section out of 4. How did you do?

Check your answers in the back of the book and write your score in the progress chart.

0–2 marks
Scan the QR code for extra practice.
Then move on to the next practice section or
try Test 10 in your Ten-Minute Tests book.

3–4 marks
Well done!
Move on to the next practice section or try
Test 10 in your Ten-Minute Tests book.

4 Complete the hexagonal grid

In each of these questions, find the image on the right that completes the pattern or sequence in the grid.

Worked example

1 Which image on the right completes the grid? Circle the correct letter.

> The grid is made of six triangles arranged into a hexagon. Each of these triangles is a separate image, and one is missing.

A   B   C   D

1 All the triangles in the grid have the same three features: a small square, a straight line, and a shaded section at the edge of the grid.

2 Each triangle has the same coloured square as the triangle opposite it, so the correct answer must have a white square. B and D can't be correct.

3 The style of the shading alternates, so the missing triangle should have dotted shading. This means C can't be correct.

4 The answer is A, because it has a white square and dotted shading.

Guided questions

1 Which image on the right completes the grid? Circle the correct letter.

> You need to read clockwise around this grid to find the pattern. Start at the top-left triangle.

A   B   C   D

1 Every triangle has a grey background. The top-left triangle has one black line and no white lines.

2 In each new triangle, there is one extra white line and one extra black line.

2 Which image on the right completes the grid? Circle the correct letter.

> This grid is made of seven hexagons. The inner hexagon may or may not be part of the pattern. You can approach it in a similar way to a grid of six triangles.

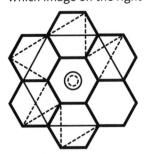

   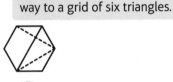

A   B   C   D

1 There is a pattern connecting the six outer hexagons. You can ignore the inner hexagon.

2 A dashed line runs through all the outer hexagons.

3 A solid line makes a hexagonal shape through the six outer hexagons.

Guided questions

1 Which image on the right completes the grid? Circle the correct letter.

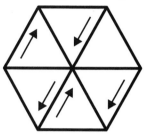

| A | B | C | D |

In a hexagonal grid, three of the triangles always point up and three always point down. This might help you work out the pattern.

1 Each triangle contains an arrow.

2 Each triangle that points down contains an arrow that points down.

2 Which image on the right completes the grid? Circle the correct letter.

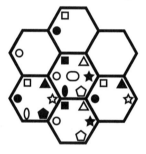

| A | B | C | D |

The number of shapes in each hexagon varies. Look for a sequence between neighbouring hexagons.

1 Start at the top-left hexagon and then read clockwise around the outside of the grid, ending with the centre hexagon.

2 When you have worked out how the number of shapes changes, look at their colours.

Have a go

1 Which image on the right completes the grid? Circle the correct letter.

| A | B | C | D |

Hexagonal grid questions will often involve more than one rule. Look at each feature in the images to make sure you have found every rule.

1

mark

Beyond the exam

There are many hexagonal patterns in nature, for example in beehives, soap bubbles and snowflakes. Try making your own paper snowflakes by taking a square sheet of paper, folding it into six and cutting shapes out of the sides. When you unfold your snowflake, look at how the pattern repeats six times.

Have a go

1 Which image on the right completes the grid? Circle the correct letter.

> If the grid has stars, look at the number of points they have and their orientation.

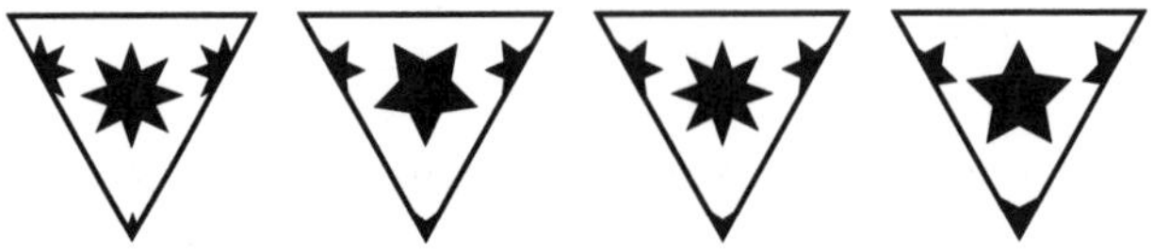

A　　　B　　　C　　　D

1 mark

2 Which image on the right completes the grid? Circle the correct letter.

> A pattern may be simpler than it looks. Compare alternating images and images opposite each other before you look for a more complicated rule.

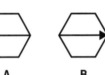

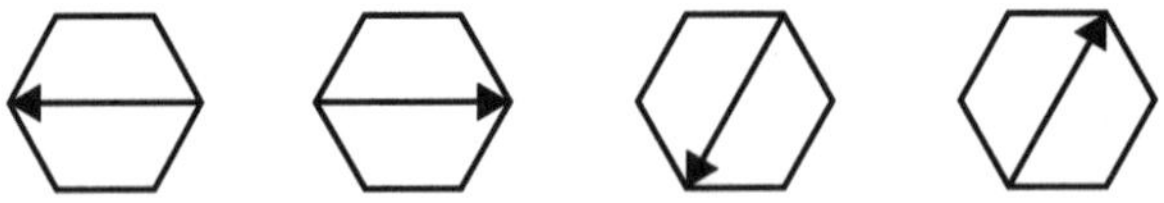

A　　　B　　　C　　　D

1 mark

3 Which image on the right completes the grid? Circle the correct letter.

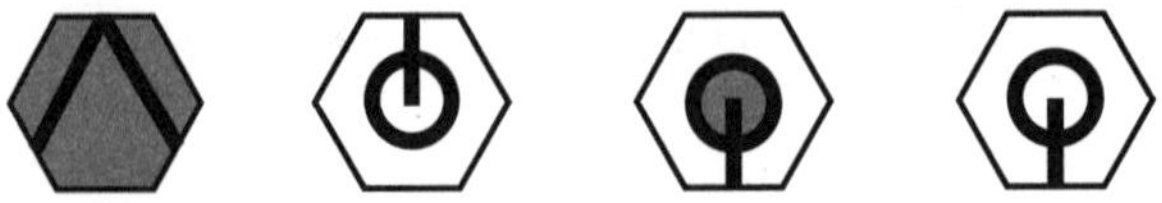

A　　　B　　　C　　　D

1 mark

Time to reflect

Mark your *Have a go* section out of 3. How are you doing so far?

Check your answers in the back of the book and see how you are doing.

Had a go 0–1 marks	**Nearly there** 2 marks	**Nailed it!** 3 marks
Have another look at the *Worked example* on page 20. Then try these questions again.	Look at your incorrect answers. Make sure you understand how to get the correct answer.	Congratulations! Now see whether you can get full marks on the *Timed practice*.

When you are ready, try the *Timed practice* on the next page.

Timed practice

3

1 Which image on the right completes the grid? Circle the correct letter.

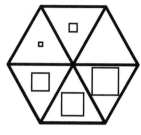

A   B   C   D

1 mark

2 Which image on the right completes the grid? Circle the correct letter.

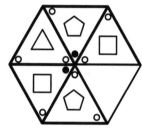

A   B   C   D

1 mark

3 Which image on the right completes the grid? Circle the correct letter.

A   B   C   D

1 mark

4 Which image on the right completes the grid? Circle the correct letter.

A   B   C   D

1 mark

Time to reflect

Mark your *Timed practice* section out of 4. How did you do?
Check your answers in the back of the book and write your score in the progress chart.

☐ *0–2 marks*
Scan the QR code for extra practice.
Then move on to the next practice section or
try Test 11 in your Ten-Minute Tests book.

☐ *3–4 marks*
Well done!
Move on to the next practice section or try
Test 11 in your Ten-Minute Tests book.

Checkpoint 1

In this checkpoint you will practise skills from the **Similarities and differences** and **Grids** topics.

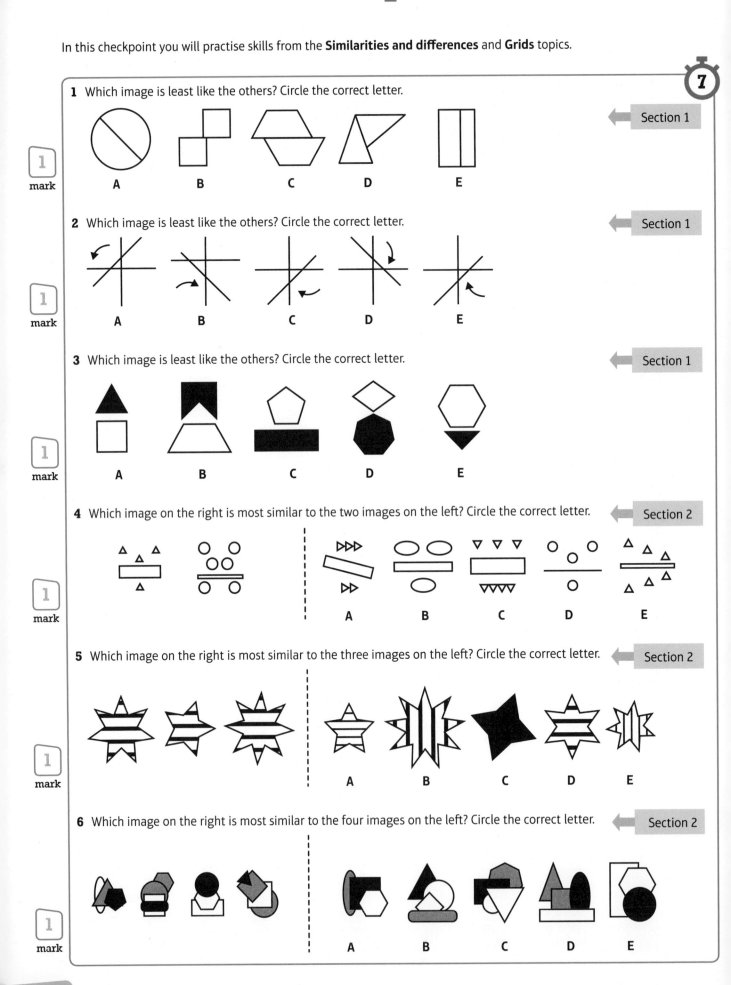

7

1 Which image is least like the others? Circle the correct letter.

Section 1

A   B   C   D   E

1 mark

2 Which image is least like the others? Circle the correct letter.

Section 1

A   B   C   D   E

1 mark

3 Which image is least like the others? Circle the correct letter.

Section 1

A   B   C   D   E

1 mark

4 Which image on the right is most similar to the two images on the left? Circle the correct letter.

Section 2

A   B   C   D   E

1 mark

5 Which image on the right is most similar to the three images on the left? Circle the correct letter.

Section 2

A   B   C   D   E

1 mark

6 Which image on the right is most similar to the four images on the left? Circle the correct letter.

Section 2

A   B   C   D   E

1 mark

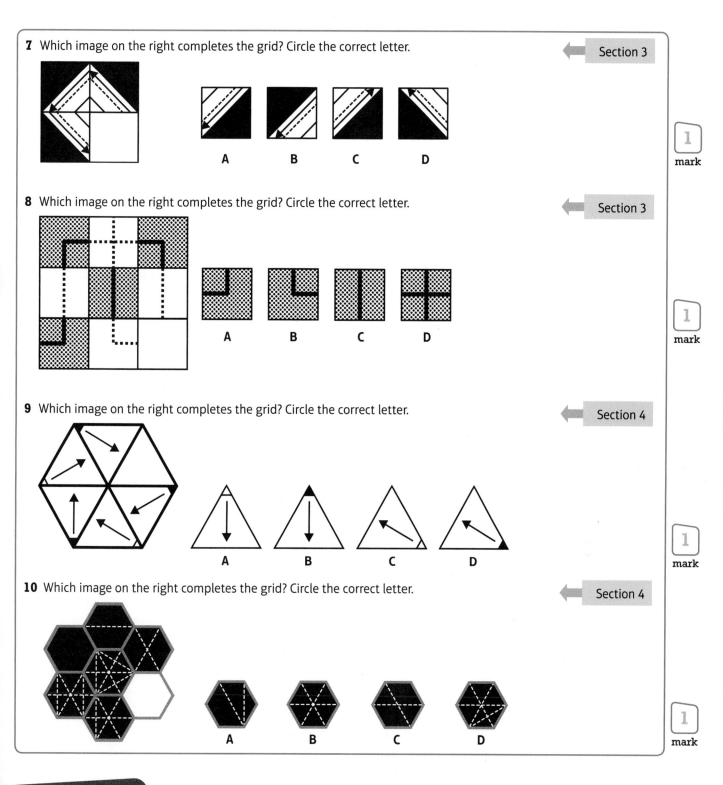

7 Which image on the right completes the grid? Circle the correct letter.

Section 3

A   B   C   D

1 mark

8 Which image on the right completes the grid? Circle the correct letter.

Section 3

A   B   C   D

1 mark

9 Which image on the right completes the grid? Circle the correct letter.

Section 4

A   B   C   D

1 mark

10 Which image on the right completes the grid? Circle the correct letter.

Section 4

A   B   C   D

1 mark

Time to reflect

Mark your *Checkpoint* out of 10. How did you do?

1 Check your answers in the back of the book and write your score in the progress chart. If any of your answers are incorrect, use the section links to find out which practice sections to look at again.

2 Scan the QR code for extra practice.

3 Move on to the next practice section.

5 Codes in boxes

In each of these questions, find which code on the right matches the final box. Each letter of the code tells you about one feature of the image. You need to work out what the code for the final image should be.

Worked example

1 Which code matches the final image? Circle the correct letter.

> The top letter tells you about one feature of the image, for example its shape, size, shading or orientation.

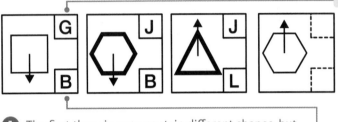

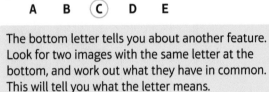

> The bottom letter tells you about another feature. Look for two images with the same letter at the bottom, and work out what they have in common. This will tell you what the letter means.

1 The first three images contain different shapes, but share some of the same letters. This means that the letters do not tell you about the type of shape.

2 The second and third images both have J in the top box. These shapes both have a thick outline, so J means a thick outline, and G means a thin outline.

3 The first and second images both have a B in the bottom box. These images both have an arrow pointing down. So B means an arrow pointing down, and L means an arrow pointing up.

4 The answer image has a shape with a thin outline and an arrow pointing up, so the top box is G and the bottom box is L. This means C is the correct answer.

Guided questions

1 Which code matches the final image? Circle the correct letter.

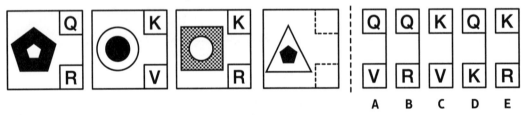

1 The first and second images are similar because the inner shape matches the outer shape. The letters of these images don't match, so this can't be part of the code.

2 In the second and third images, the inner shape is a circle and the top letter is K, so the top box tells you what the inner shape is. Compare the final image with the other images to work out the top letter of the code.

3 Each inner shape is either black or white. Look at the letters in the bottom boxes to work out which means black and which means white.

2 Which code matches the final image? Circle the correct letter.

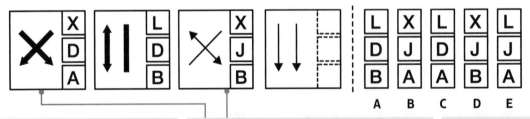

In this question there are three letters. Use the same steps as before, but look for three things that change instead of two.	The first and third images have the same top letter and both contain crossed lines. So X must mean that the lines are crossed. Look for other similarities to find the other letters.	The letters don't stand for anything. In this puzzle, X means the lines are crossed, but not because X looks like a cross.

Guided questions

1 Which code matches the final image? Circle the correct letter.

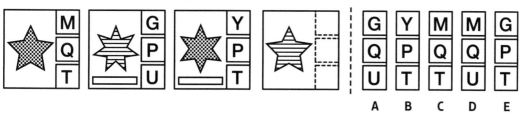

A B C D E

Each image contains a star, but the shading of the star varies. Some images also contain a rectangle.

Each of the top boxes contains a different letter, so there must be something different in all three images.

2 Which code matches the final image? Circle the correct letter.

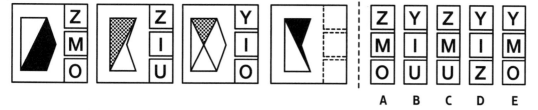

A B C D E

These images are more complex, but you should approach the question in the same way as the others. Think about the outer shape and how many different sections each image has.

Have a go

A letter can tell you whether or not something is in the image.

1 Which code matches the final image? Circle the correct letter.

A B C D E

1
mark

Look for small differences in patterns, such as the style of the shading.

2 Which code matches the final image? Circle the correct letter.

    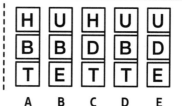

A B C D E

1
mark

Beyond the exam

Make up your own code game using a pack of playing cards. Choose five different letters and give each one a rule. For example, A – odd numbers, B – red cards, C – picture cards, D – prime numbers, E – diamonds. Keep your code secret and get a partner to turn over the cards one at a time. Say the letters that each card matches. See how many cards it takes for your partner to guess the rules.

Have a go

1 Which code matches the final image? Circle the correct letter.

If an image is very simple, try looking at what changes in it and comparing that to the letters.

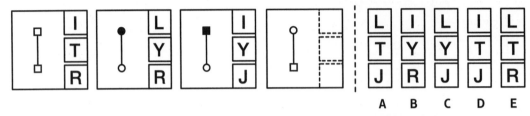

A   B   C   D   E

1 mark

2 Which code matches the final image? Circle the correct letter.

If the images all have the same shapes, think about the size, colour and position of the shapes.

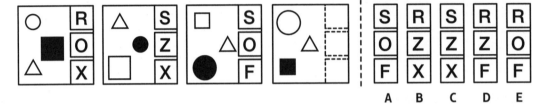

A   B   C   D   E

1 mark

3 Which code matches the final image? Circle the correct letter.

Remember to count features of the images.

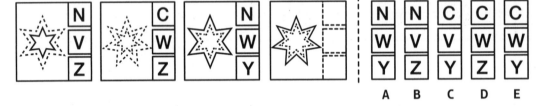

A   B   C   D   E

1 mark

4 Which code matches the final image? Circle the correct letter.

Think about combinations of shapes.

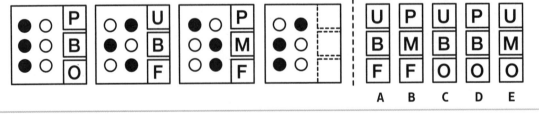

A   B   C   D   E

1 mark

Time to reflect

Mark your *Have a go* section out of 4. How are you doing so far?

Check your answers in the back of the book and see how you are doing.

Had a go	**Nearly there**	**Nailed it!**
0–1 marks	*2–3 marks*	*4 marks*
Have another look at the *Worked example* on page 26. Then try these questions again.	Look at your incorrect answers. Make sure you understand how to get the correct answer.	Congratulations! Now see whether you can get full marks on the *Timed practice*.

When you are ready, try the *Timed practice* on the next page.

Timed practice

4

1 Which code matches the final image? Circle the correct letter.

   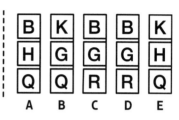

B	K	B	B	K
H	G	G	G	H
Q	Q	R	R	Q
A	**B**	**C**	**D**	**E**

1 mark

2 Which code matches the final image? Circle the correct letter.

    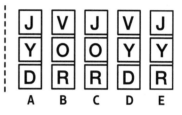

J	V	J	V	J
Y	O	O	Y	Y
D	R	R	D	R
A	**B**	**C**	**D**	**E**

1 mark

3 Which code matches the final image? Circle the correct letter.

    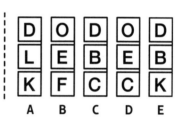

D	O	D	O	D
L	E	B	E	B
K	F	C	C	K
A	**B**	**C**	**D**	**E**

1 mark

4 Which code matches the final image? Circle the correct letter.

    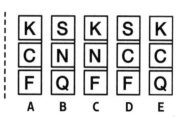

K	S	K	S	K
C	N	N	C	C
F	Q	F	F	Q
A	**B**	**C**	**D**	**E**

1 mark

5 Which code matches the final image? Circle the correct letter.

    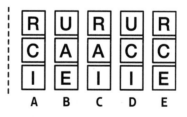

R	U	R	U	R
C	A	A	C	C
I	E	I	I	E
A	**B**	**C**	**D**	**E**

1 mark

Time to reflect

Mark your *Timed practice* section out of 5. How did you do?

Check your answers in the back of the book and write your score in the progress chart.

☐ *0–3 marks*
Scan the QR code for extra practice.
Then move on to the next practice section or
try Test 13 in your Ten-Minute Tests book.

☐ *4–5 marks*
Well done!
Move on to the next practice section or try
Test 13 in your Ten-Minute Tests book.

6 Codes in lists

Each image in these questions has a code underneath it, apart from the final image. Each letter of the code tells you about one feature of the image. You need to work out what the code for the final image should be.

Worked example

1 Which code matches the final image? Circle the correct letter.

The left letter and the right letter tell you about two different features of the image.

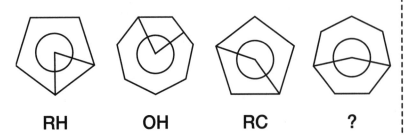

RH   OH   RC   ?

RC   RH   OH   OC   RC
A   B   C   (D)   E

① The first and third images both have R for the first letter. They also both have five sides. So the first letter tells you how many sides the outer shape has. R means five sides and O means seven sides.

② The first and second images both have H as the second letter. They also both have a vertex at the bottom. So the second letter tells you the orientation of the outer shape. C means it has a vertex at the top, and H means it has a vertex at the bottom.

③ The outer shape in the final image has seven sides and a vertex at the top, so the code is OC. The answer is D.

Guided questions

1 Which code matches the final image? Circle the correct letter.

Look at the features and how they change. The arrows in these images all point anticlockwise, so this feature is not part of the code.

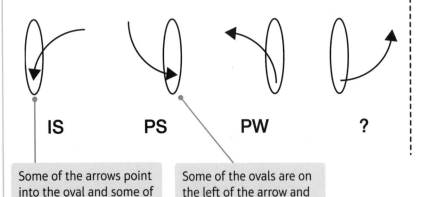

IS   PS   PW   ?

IS   IW   PS   PW   PI
A   B   C   D   E

Some of the arrows point into the oval and some of them point out of it.

Some of the ovals are on the left of the arrow and some are on the right.

2 Which code matches the final image? Circle the correct letter.

Look for a connection between the letters and the number of arrowheads in each image.

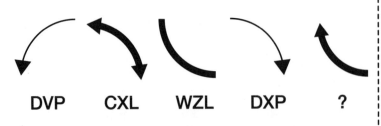

DVP   CXL   WZL   DXP   ?

DZL CVP CZL WVP WXL
A   B   C   D   E

Guided questions

1 Which code matches the final image? Circle the correct letter.

Think about features such as the type, number, shading, orientation and position of the triangles.

FMJ   ALJ   FLK   ?

FLJ	FMK	AMJ	ALJ	AMK
A	B	C	D	E

1 The first and third images both have the same first letter and both contain three triangles.

2 The second and third images both have the same second letter and contain only isosceles triangles.

2 Which code matches the final image? Circle the correct letter.

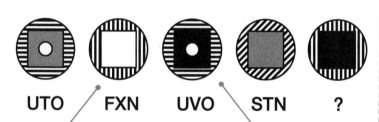

UTO   FXN   UVO   STN   ?

FTO	FVN	UXO	SVO	SXN
A	B	C	D	E

If an image has line shading, look carefully at the direction of the lines. They might be horizontal, vertical or diagonal.

Each image contains a shaded circle and a square. Some also contain a small white circle.

Have a go

1 Which code matches the final image? Circle the correct letter.

If the code has three letters, look for three different features.

JDF   IDT   JOT   ?

JOT	IDT	JOF	IOT	JDF
A	B	C	D	E

1 mark

2 Which code matches the final image? Circle the correct letter.

Look at where the shapes are in relation to each other.

LKH   LNG   TNZ   IYZ   ?

LNH	TYZ	TYG	TNH	IYZ
A	B	C	D	E

1 mark

Have a go

1 Which code matches the final image? Circle the correct letter.

Look carefully at any overlapping shapes to see which order they overlap in.

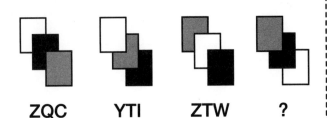

ZQC   YTI   ZTW   ?

ZQW   ZTI   YQW   YTC   ZYI
A   B   C   D   E

1 mark

2 Which code matches the final image? Circle the correct letter.

For three-letter codes, write down each letter as you work it out to help you remember it.

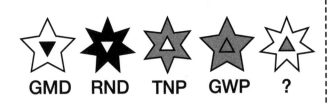

GMD   RND   TNP   GWP   ?

GNP TMD TWD RMP RWP
A   B   C   D   E

1 mark

3 Which code matches the final image? Circle the correct letter.

Remember to look at the directions the arrows point in.

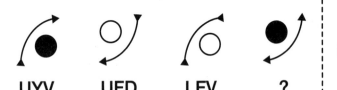

UYV   UFD   LFV   ?

LFD   UFV   UYD   LYV   LYD
A   B   C   D   E

1 mark

4 Which code matches the final image? Circle the correct letter.

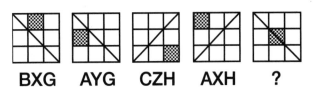

BXG   AYG   CZH   AXH   ?

BXH AZG AYH BYG CZG
A   B   C   D   E

1 mark

Time to reflect

Mark your *Have a go* section out of 4. How are you doing so far?

Check your answers in the back of the book and see how you are doing.

Had a go	**Nearly there**	**Nailed it!**
0–1 marks	*2–3 marks*	*4 marks*

Have another look at the *Worked example* on page 30. Then try these questions again.

Look at your incorrect answers. Make sure you understand how to get the correct answer.

Congratulations! Now see whether you can get full marks on the *Timed practice*.

When you are ready, try the *Timed practice* on the next page.

Timed practice

1 Which code matches the final image? Circle the correct letter.

MU   QR   MR   ?

QR	QU	MV	MR	MU
A	B	C	D	E

1 mark

2 Which code matches the final image? Circle the correct letter.

DOG   TON   DAB   ?

TAG	TOG	TUB	DAN	DON
A	B	C	D	E

1 mark

3 Which code matches the final image? Circle the correct letter.

HYM   EWO   HWO   ELM   ?

HLM	EYM	HWO	EWO	HYO
A	B	C	D	E

1 mark

4 Which code matches the final image? Circle the correct letter.

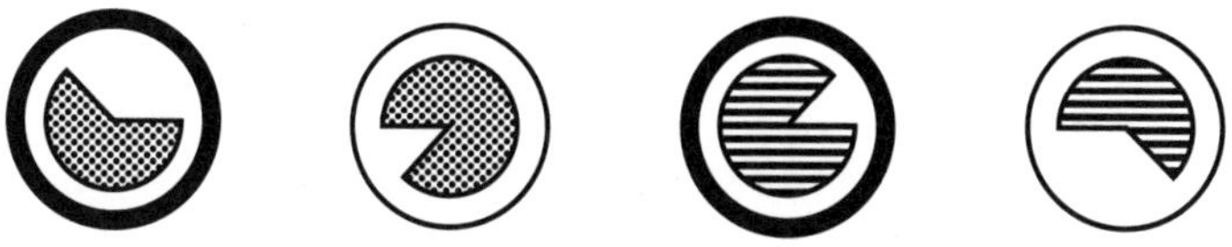

GNV   JNC   GAC   ?

GAV	GNV	JAV	JAC	JNC
A	B	C	D	E

1 mark

5 Which code matches the final image? Circle the correct letter.

ADG   BEH   BDI   CFI   ?

CDI	CEG	BEG	AEI	BEI
A	B	C	D	E

1 mark

Time to reflect

Mark your *Timed practice* section out of 5. How did you do?
Check your answers in the back of the book and write your score in the progress chart.

☐   *0–3 marks*
Scan the QR code for extra practice.
Then move on to the next practice section or
try Test 15 in your Ten-Minute Tests book.

☐   *4–5 marks*
Well done!
Move on to the next practice section or try
Test 15 in your Ten-Minute Tests book.

Checkpoint 2

In this checkpoint you will practise skills from the **Codes** topic.

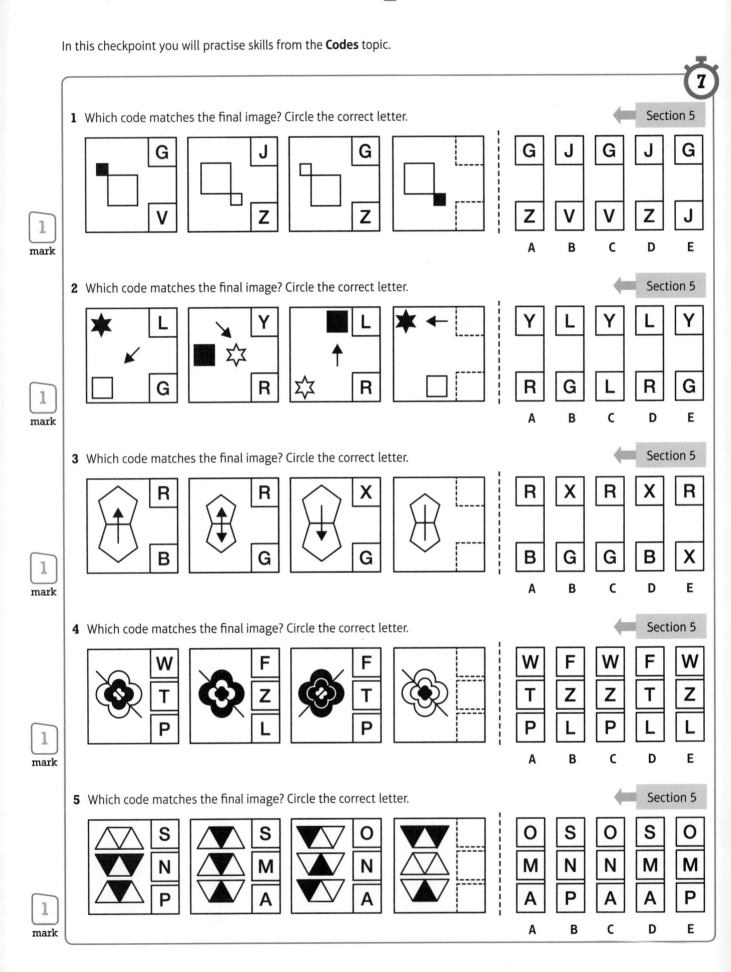

1 Which code matches the final image? Circle the correct letter.

Section 5

1 mark

2 Which code matches the final image? Circle the correct letter.

Section 5

1 mark

3 Which code matches the final image? Circle the correct letter.

Section 5

1 mark

4 Which code matches the final image? Circle the correct letter.

Section 5

1 mark

5 Which code matches the final image? Circle the correct letter.

Section 5

1 mark

6 Which code matches the final image? Circle the correct letter.

← Section 6

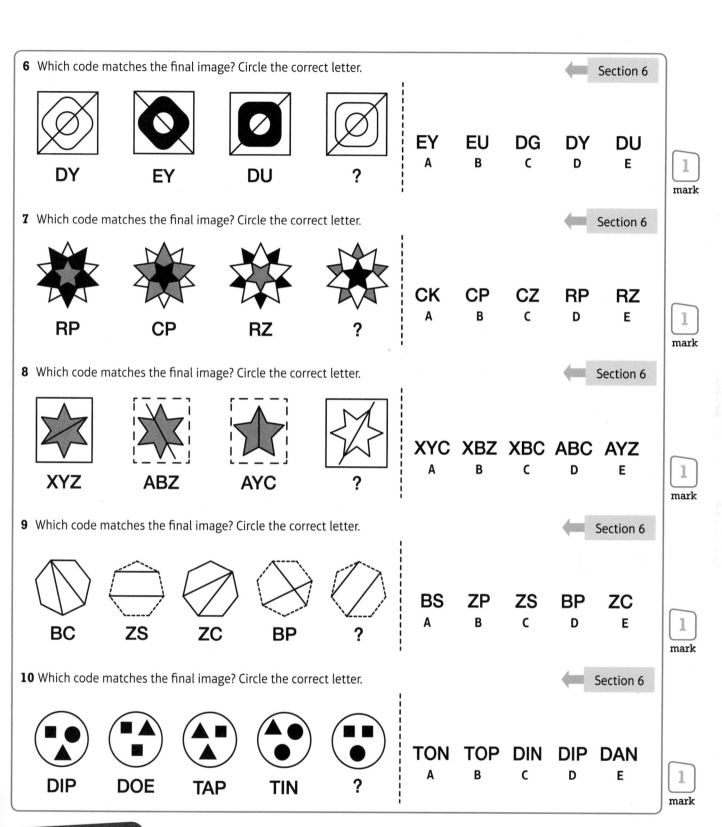

EY   EU   DG   DY   DU
A   B   C   D   E

1 mark

7 Which code matches the final image? Circle the correct letter.

← Section 6

CK   CP   CZ   RP   RZ
A   B   C   D   E

1 mark

8 Which code matches the final image? Circle the correct letter.

← Section 6

XYC   XBZ   XBC   ABC   AYZ
A   B   C   D   E

1 mark

9 Which code matches the final image? Circle the correct letter.

← Section 6

BS   ZP   ZS   BP   ZC
A   B   C   D   E

1 mark

10 Which code matches the final image? Circle the correct letter.

← Section 6

TON   TOP   DIN   DIP   DAN
A   B   C   D   E

1 mark

Time to reflect

Mark your *Checkpoint* out of 10. How did you do?

1 Check your answers in the back of the book and write your score in the progress chart. If any of your answers are incorrect, use the section links to find out which practice sections to look at again.

2 Scan the QR code for extra practice.

3 Move on to the next practice section.

7 Which cube does not match the net?

Each of these questions shows you a net and five cubes. Four of the cubes can be made by folding up the net. Look at the patterns to work out which cube cannot be made by folding up the net.

Worked example

1 Which cube cannot be made from the net on the left? Circle the correct letter.

Imagine folding up the net into a cube. If you turned it around, you would be able to see all of the cubes except for one.

A   B   C   D   E

The net has six different faces.

You can see three faces on each of the cubes, so for each cube you only need to look at three patterns on the net.

C has two triangle faces, and the net only has one. C is the answer.

Guided questions

1 Which cube cannot be made from the net on the left? Circle the correct letter.

The faces on this net are arranged differently, but it will still fold up to make a cube. Make sure you know all the ways the net could be laid out.

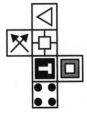

A   B   C   D   E

1 Imagine folding up the net. The faces with the crossed arrows and the triangle would be next to each other because they touch at one corner on the net.

2 The point of the triangle should be next to the arrowheads, like on cube D.

3 Find a cube where this is not the case.

2 Which cube cannot be made from the net on the left? Circle the correct letter.

Look for shapes that point in a particular direction, such as arrows or triangles.

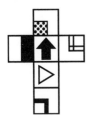

A   B   C   D   E

1 The arrow on the net points towards the face with the dotted square and away from the face with the triangle.

2 Look at each cube that has an arrow. Check that the arrow is pointing in the correct direction.

Guided questions

1 Which cube cannot be made from the net on the left? Circle the correct letter.

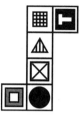

A   B   C   D   E

> Think carefully about how the faces will connect when the net is folded up. The black circle and the grid are far apart on the net, but would touch on the folded cube.

1 You can see three faces on each of the cubes. Find these faces on the net and see if they would fold up in the same way.

2 Work out which faces on the net would be opposite each other. Check that they are not next to each another on any of the cubes.

2 Which cube cannot be made from the net on the left? Circle the correct letter.

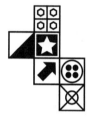

A   B   C   D   E

> Think about which faces would be next to each other and how the orientation of the shapes would change when the net was folded.

1 Look for a shape that looks different when it is rotated. This makes it easier to tell if it is incorrect on any of the cubes.

2 The star has one point towards the grid and two points towards the arrow. Check that it has the correct orientation on each of the cubes.

Have a go

1 Which cube cannot be made from the net on the left? Circle the correct letter.

A   B   C   D   E

> Start by checking that all the faces on the cubes appear on the net.

> 1 mark

2 Which cube cannot be made from the net on the left? Circle the correct letter.

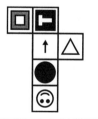

A   B   C   D   E

> Only one cube will be wrong, so once you have found it you do not need to check that the others are right.

> 1 mark

Beyond the exam

Use a ruler to draw as many different cube nets as you can think of. Look at this section and the next to help you come up with ideas. There are eleven different nets in total – see if you can draw them all.

Have a go

1 Which cube cannot be made from the net on the left? Circle the correct letter.

A B C D E

1 mark

> Choose two faces that share a side on both the net and a cube. Check that they are arranged in the same way on both.

2 Which cube cannot be made from the net on the left? Circle the correct letter.

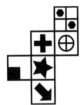

A B C D E

1 mark

> Sometimes the cubes can help you work out the answer. You know that only one cube is wrong. So if two cubes show the same faces sharing a side, then those faces must be correct because at least one of those cubes is correct.

3 Which cube cannot be made from the net on the left? Circle the correct letter.

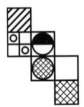

A B C D E

1 mark

> If you find two cubes showing the same two faces arranged differently, then one of those cubes must be incorrect.

4 Which cube cannot be made from the net on the left? Circle the correct letter.

A B C D E

1 mark

Time to reflect

Mark your *Have a go* section out of 4. How are you doing so far?

Check your answers in the back of the book and see how you are doing.

☐ **Had a go**
0–1 marks

☐ **Nearly there**
2–3 marks

☐ **Nailed it!**
4 marks

Have another look at the *Worked example* on page 36. Then try these questions again.

Look at your incorrect answers. Make sure you understand how to get the correct answer.

Congratulations! Now see whether you can get full marks on the *Timed practice*.

When you are ready, try the *Timed practice* on the next page.

Timed practice

1 Which cube cannot be made from the net on the left? Circle the correct letter.

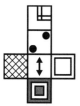

A   B   C   D   E

1 mark

2 Which cube cannot be made from the net on the left? Circle the correct letter.

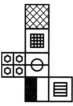

A   B   C   D   E

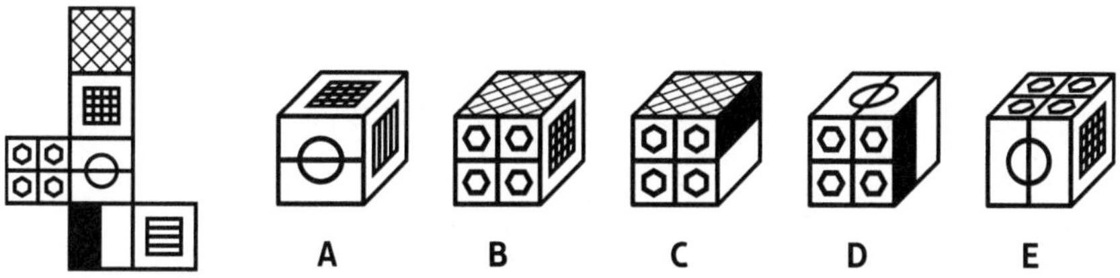

1 mark

3 Which cube cannot be made from the net on the left? Circle the correct letter.

A   B   C   D   E

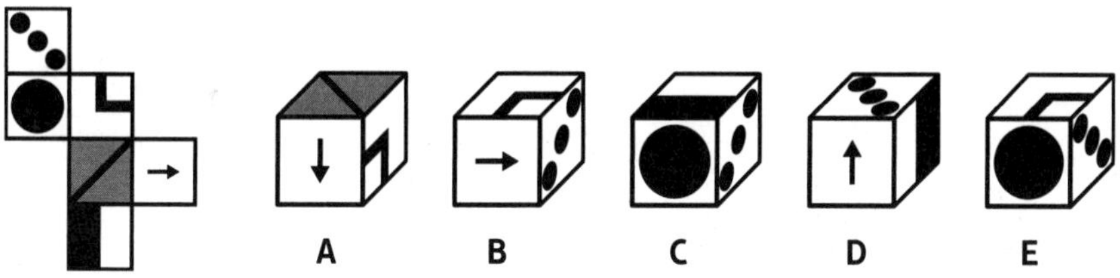

1 mark

4 Which cube cannot be made from the net on the left? Circle the correct letter.

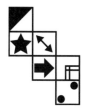

A   B   C   D   E

1 mark

5 Which cube cannot be made from the net on the left? Circle the correct letter.

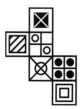

A   B   C   D   E

1 mark

Time to reflect

Mark your *Timed practice* section out of 5. How did you do?

Check your answers in the back of the book and write your score in the progress chart.

☐ **0–3 marks**

Scan the QR code for extra practice.
Then move on to the next practice section or try Test 18 in your Ten-Minute Tests book.

☐ **4–5 marks**

Well done!
Move on to the next practice section or try Test 18 in your Ten-Minute Tests book.

8 Which net matches the cube?

In each of these questions, find which net can be folded to make the cube on the left.

Worked example

1 Which net makes the cube on the left? Circle the correct letter.

> You can only see three faces on the cube, so you only need to look at those three patterns on each net.

          A   **B**   **C**   **D**

1 The correct net must include all three of the faces shown on the cube. A has a white face instead of a grey face, so it must be incorrect.

2 Look at how the faces touch. On the cube, the single arrow, the double arrow and the grey face are all touching. In D, the grey face and the single arrow are on opposite faces, so it is incorrect.

3 Look at the direction of the shapes on the cube. The arrows are all pointing away from the grey face. If you folded up B, the double arrow would be pointing towards the grey face, so this net is incorrect.

4 C must be the correct net.

Guided questions

1 Which net makes the cube on the left? Circle the correct letter.

> Check that each of the nets can make a cube. Some might fold up incorrectly or have the wrong number of faces.

          A   **B**   **C**   **D**

1 Check that each net has the three faces shown on the cube. B has two dots instead of three, so it must be incorrect.

2 Look at the faces that are touching on the cube and which way around they are. The top of the T is next to the three dots, and the black triangle is next to the left side of the T. Use this to help you find the answer.

2 Which net makes the cube on the left? Circle the correct letter.

  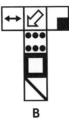 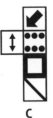 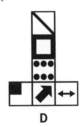

          A   **B**   **C**   **D**

1 On the cube, the small black square is touching the face with six dots. Cross out any nets where the black square would not touch the dotted face.

2 On the cube, the black arrow points to the dotted face. Cross out any nets where this would not be the case.

Guided questions

1 Which net makes the cube on the left? Circle the correct letter.

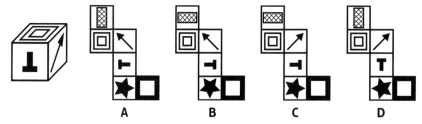

A   B   C   D

1 Look for faces that will look different if they are rotated. The squares will look the same whichever way the cube is turned, so concentrate on the T and the arrow.

2 The arrow on the cube starts near the top of the T and points diagonally towards the square. Find the net that has the arrow in the same position.

2 Which net makes the cube on the left? Circle the correct letter.

    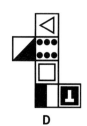

A   B   C   D

If a net has four squares in a column, you can rearrange the faces on either side to make the familiar cross shape shown by net A. Imagine rolling a face up or down the side of the column. It will rotate 90° clockwise if you roll it one space clockwise, or 90° anticlockwise if you roll it one space anticlockwise.

Have a go

1 Which net makes the cube on the left? Circle the correct letter.

 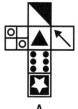 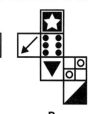 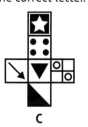 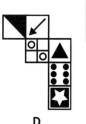

A   B   C   D

Imagine folding up each net. If any of the faces overlap, you can cross it out.

mark

2 Which net makes the cube on the left? Circle the correct letter.

A   B   C   D

If all three faces appear in the correct place on the net, compare how they are rotated to find the answer.

mark

Beyond the exam

Choose an unusually shaped net from this section. Use a ruler to draw it onto paper or card. Cut your net out and see which faces are next to each other when you fold it into a cube.

Have a go

1 Which net makes the cube on the left? Circle the correct letter.

    A   **B**   **C**   **D**

1 mark

> Check that the faces on the cube are exactly the same on the nets. If the colours have changed or the lines are the wrong thickness, you know the net is incorrect.

2 Which net makes the cube on the left? Circle the correct letter.

 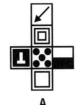  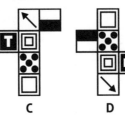

    A   **B**   **C**   **D**

1 mark

> Think about how a shape might look if it has been rotated.

3 Which net makes the cube on the left? Circle the correct letter.

 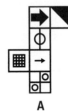  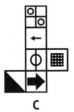 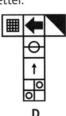

    A   **B**   **C**   **D**

1 mark

> If the cube has any arrows on it, start with these. It is easy to check if they have been rotated.

4 Which net makes the cube on the left? Circle the correct letter.

 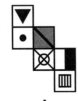  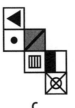 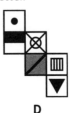

    A   **B**   **C**   **D**

1 mark

Time to reflect

Mark your *Have a go* section out of 4. How are you doing so far?

Check your answers in the back of the book and see how you are doing.

☐ **Had a go**	☐ **Nearly there**	☐ **Nailed it!**
0–1 marks	*2–3 marks*	*4 marks*
Have another look at the *Worked example* on page 40. Then try these questions again.	Look at your incorrect answers. Make sure you understand how to get the correct answer.	Congratulations! Now see whether you can get full marks on the *Timed practice*.

When you are ready, try the *Timed practice* on the next page.

Timed practice

🕐 4

1 Which net makes the cube on the left? Circle the correct letter.

 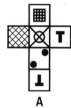 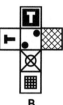  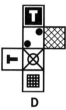

                A   **B**   **C**   **D**

2 Which net makes the cube on the left? Circle the correct letter.

                A   **B**   **C**   **D**

3 Which net makes the cube on the left? Circle the correct letter.

    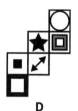

                A   **B**   **C**   **D**

4 Which net makes the cube on the left? Circle the correct letter.

 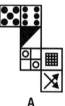  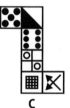 

                A   **B**   **C**   **D**

5 Which net makes the cube on the left? Circle the correct letter.

 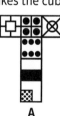 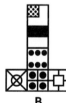 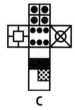 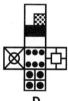

                A   **B**   **C**   **D**

Time to reflect

Mark your *Timed practice* section out of 5. How did you do?
Check your answers in the back of the book and write your score in the progress chart.

☐ *0–3 marks*
   Scan the QR code for extra practice.
Then move on to the next practice section or
try Test 19 in your Ten-Minute Tests book.

☐ *4–5 marks*
   Well done!
Move on to the next practice section or try
Test 19 in your Ten-Minute Tests book.

9 Non-cube nets

In each of these questions, find which net makes the 3D solid on the left.

Worked example

1 Which net makes the 3D solid on the left? Circle the correct letter.

Some of these net options won't make the correct 3D solid. Others will have the wrong patterns on the faces.

 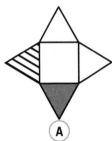 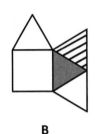 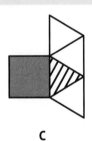 

A   B   C   D

1 This 3D solid is a square-based pyramid. To make this 3D solid, the net must have one square face and four triangular faces. When folded up, each side of the square face must touch a different triangular face.

2 B and C both have triangular sides that would not touch the square face when folded. They are incorrect.

3 The 3D solid has a triangular grey face and a triangular striped face next to each another. Net D has both these patterns, but the striped face is square. So D can't be correct.

4 The answer must be A.

Guided question

1 Which net makes the 3D solid on the left? Circle the correct letter.

All of these nets will create a cuboid when folded, so you need to look at the patterns on the faces to find the correct answer.

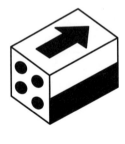 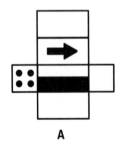 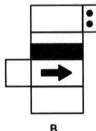 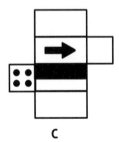 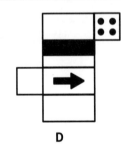

A   B   C   D

1 On the 3D solid, the face with the arrow is touching the white half of the face with the black and white rectangles. On the correct net, the arrow must be next to the white rectangle.

2 On the 3D solid, the arrow points away from the square face with dots on it.

3 Cross out all of the nets that do not have these features to find the correct answer.

Beyond the exam

Look for objects with interesting shapes, such as a chocolate box, a pencil case, or a baked bean tin. Imagine what the net for each object would look like. Then try drawing your nets and cutting them out to see if you were correct.

Guided questions

1 Which net makes the 3D solid on the left? Circle the correct letter.

123 This 3D solid is a hexagonal prism. This means it is made of two hexagons and six quadrilaterals. Different kinds of prism have different shapes on the end, for example, triangular prisms, pentagonal prisms or heptagonal prisms.

 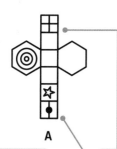 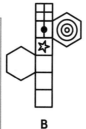 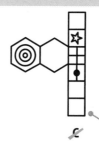 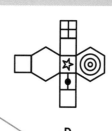

A   B   C   D

Look at the orientation of the patterns to help you work out which net is correct. The top point of the star should point to the circles.

Remember that the square faces at the top and bottom will be next to each other when the net is folded up.

A, B and D will make a hexagonal prism, but C will not. Cross out option C.

2 Which net makes the 3D solid on the left? Circle the correct letter.

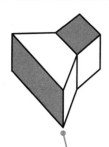 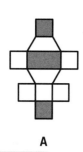 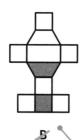 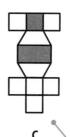 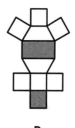

A   B   C   D

Try splitting complex 3D solids into simpler ones. For example, this one is made from a cube and a trapezium-based prism.

The correct net needs a grey rectangular face. B does not have one, so you can cross it out.

Check that the faces on each net will not overlap when they are folded up. If they do, there will be gaps in other places.

3 Which net makes the 3D solid on the left? Circle the correct letter.

Remember that faces on the back of the 3D solid might be a different shape from the ones you can see.

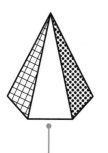    

A   B   C   D

Check that the patterned faces are in the correct places on the nets.

Remember to imagine the net folding away from you, so that the patterns are on the outside.

Have a go

1 Which net makes the 3D solid on the left? Circle the correct letter.

> Make sure any shaded or patterned faces will be in the correct place when each net is folded up.

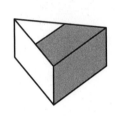 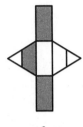 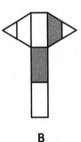 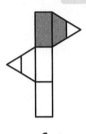 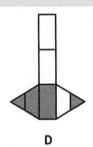

A   B   C   D

1 mark

2 Which net makes the 3D solid on the left? Circle the correct letter.

> If the 3D solid is a prism, check that the faces at the ends of the prism are at opposite sides of the square or rectangular faces. If they are on the same side, the net will not work.

A   B   C   D

1 mark

3 Which net makes the 3D solid on the left? Circle the correct letter.

> If all the nets are exactly the same shape, focus on the patterns instead. Work out which order the grey and white faces should appear in.

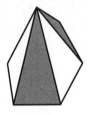    

A   B   C   D

1 mark

Time to reflect

Mark your *Have a go* section out of 3. How are you doing so far?

Check your answers in the back of the book and see how you are doing.

Had a go 0–1 marks	**Nearly there** 2 marks	**Nailed it!** 3 marks
Have another look at the *Worked example* on page 44. Then try these questions again.	Look at your incorrect answer. Make sure you understand how to get the correct answer.	Congratulations! Now see whether you can get full marks on the *Timed practice*.

When you are ready, try the *Timed practice* on the next page.

Timed practice

③

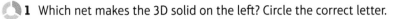

1 Which net makes the 3D solid on the left? Circle the correct letter.

        A   **B**   **C**   **D**

1 mark

2 Which net makes the 3D solid on the left? Circle the correct letter.

        A   **B**   **C**   **D**

1 mark

3 Which net makes the 3D solid on the left? Circle the correct letter.

  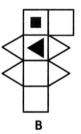 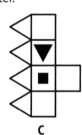 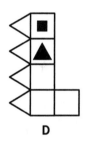

        A   **B**   **C**   **D**

1 mark

4 Which net makes the 3D solid on the left? Circle the correct letter.

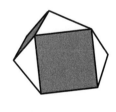    

        A   **B**   **C**   **D**

1 mark

Time to reflect

Mark your *Timed practice* section out of 4. How did you do?

Check your answers in the back of the book and write your score in the progress chart.

☐ *0–2 marks*
   Scan the QR code for extra practice.
Then move on to the next practice section or
try Test 20 in your Ten-Minute Tests book.

☐ *3–4 marks*
   Well done!
Move on to the next practice section or try
Test 20 in your Ten-Minute Tests book.

Checkpoint 3

In this checkpoint you will practise skills from the **Nets** topic.

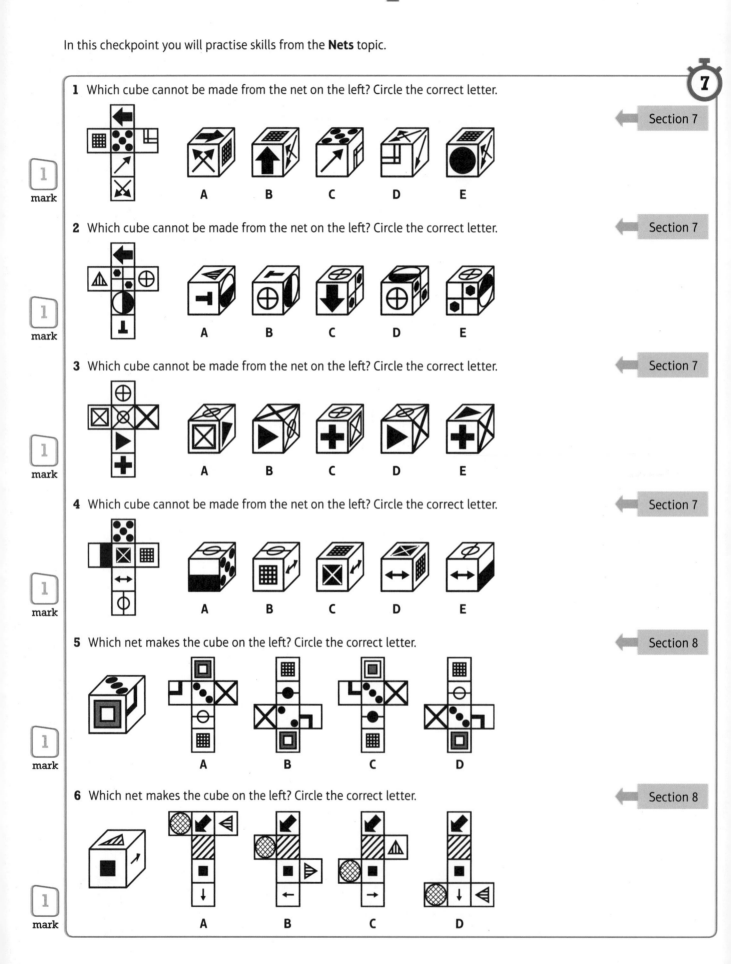

1 Which cube cannot be made from the net on the left? Circle the correct letter.

Section 7

A   B   C   D   E

1 mark

2 Which cube cannot be made from the net on the left? Circle the correct letter.

Section 7

A   B   C   D   E

1 mark

3 Which cube cannot be made from the net on the left? Circle the correct letter.

Section 7

A   B   C   D   E

1 mark

4 Which cube cannot be made from the net on the left? Circle the correct letter.

Section 7

A   B   C   D   E

1 mark

5 Which net makes the cube on the left? Circle the correct letter.

Section 8

A   B   C   D

1 mark

6 Which net makes the cube on the left? Circle the correct letter.

Section 8

A   B   C   D

1 mark

7 Which net makes the cube on the left? Circle the correct letter. ← Section 8

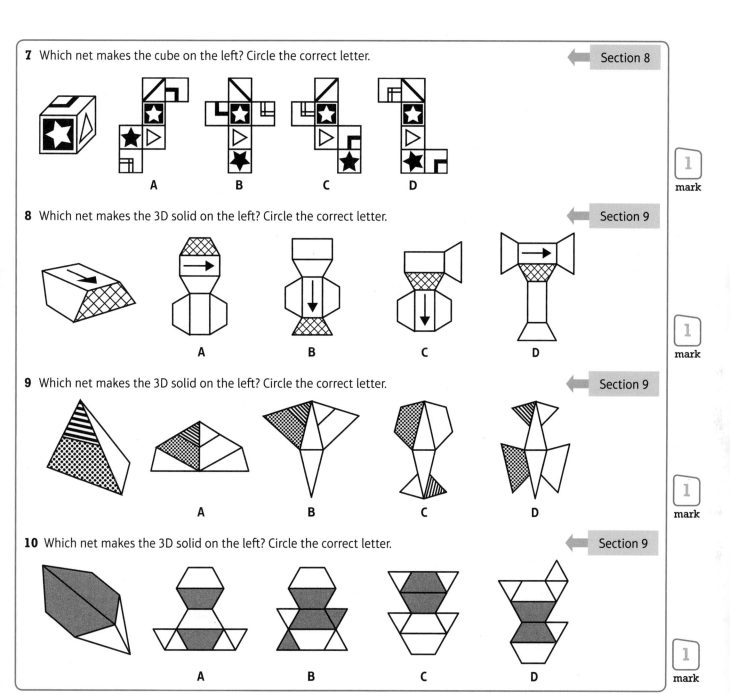

A   B   C   D

1 mark

8 Which net makes the 3D solid on the left? Circle the correct letter. ← Section 9

A   B   C   D

1 mark

9 Which net makes the 3D solid on the left? Circle the correct letter. ← Section 9

A   B   C   D

1 mark

10 Which net makes the 3D solid on the left? Circle the correct letter. ← Section 9

A   B   C   D

1 mark

Time to reflect

Mark your *Checkpoint* out of 10. How did you do?

1 Check your answers in the back of the book and write your score in the progress chart. If any of your answers are incorrect, use the section links to find out which practice sections to look at again.

2 Scan the QR code for extra practice.

3 Move on to the next practice section.

10 2D views of 3D solids

In each of these questions, the image on the left is a 3D solid made of cubes. Decide which 2D shape on the right it would look like when viewed from the direction shown by the arrow.

Worked example

1 Which image is a view of the 3D solid on the left from the direction of the arrow? Circle the correct letter.

> The arrow tells you which direction you need to look at the 3D solid from.

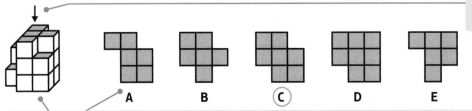

A B (C) D E

The arrow is pointing down from above, so the correct answer shows a top-down view of the 3D solid. The bottom row of squares in each 2D image represents the front row of cubes in the 3D solid.

① Look at the front row of the 3D solid. There are two cubes in the front row, so there should be two squares in the bottom row of the 2D view. B and E must be wrong.

② There are no spaces in the middle row of the 3D solid, so the middle row of the 2D view must have three squares. A is wrong.

③ The back row of the 3D solid has cubes in the middle column and no cubes in the right column. You can't tell whether it has cubes in the left column. D must be wrong because it has a square in the top right, so C is the answer.

Guided questions

1 Which image is a view of the 3D solid on the left from the direction of the arrow? Circle the correct letter.

> Imagine you are standing in the position of the arrow and looking in the direction it is pointing. The cubes on your left will be in the left column of the 2D view.

A B C D E

① Start with the nearest row of cubes on the 3D solid. They are the easiest to see.

② The nearest row will look like a column with only one cube in it when viewed from the side.

③ This column will be the left column in the 2D view. Look for the answer with one square in the left column.

2 Which image is a view of the 3D solid on the left from the direction of the arrow? Circle the correct letter.

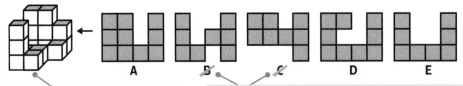

A B C D E

> These cubes are arranged in four rows. The arrow is pointing left.

> There is at least one cube in every bottom row. This means that there must be no gaps in the bottom row of the answer, so B and C are wrong. Work out where the other gaps should be to help you find the answer.

Beyond the exam

Look at each of the solids on this page. Some of them might have cubes that are out of sight. Work out the maximum and minimum number of cubes that would be needed to construct the solid.

Guided questions

1 Which image is a view of the 3D solid on the left from the direction of the arrow? Circle the correct letter.

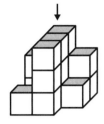

A B C D E

1 The columns on the right of the 3D solid are easiest to see. There is one gap on the right, so just one of the right-hand squares in the 2D view should be empty. This lets you cross out two options.

2 There is also a gap on the left of the 3D solid. Use this to help you find the answer.

> The closest row of cubes in the 3D solid is on the left of the 2D views. Work out how many cubes are in these columns, and use this to cross out three options.

2 Which image is a view of the 3D solid on the left from the direction of the arrow? Circle the correct letter.

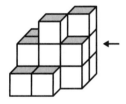 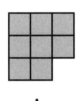

A B C D E

3 Which image is a view of the 3D solid on the left from the direction of the arrow? Circle the correct letter.

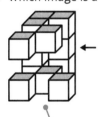 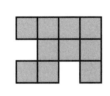   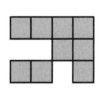

A B C D E

> This solid has floating cubes. Look carefully at the cubes around them to work out where they fit.

> Count how many cubes you can see at the top of the 3D solid to work out how many squares will be in the top row of the 2D view. Remember that some cubes will be behind others.

Have a go

> In top-down views, the height of the columns doesn't matter. If there is a cube in any row or column of the 3D solid, there should be a square in the same place in the 2D view.

1 Which image is a view of the 3D solid on the left from the direction of the arrow? Circle the correct letter.

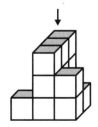

A B C D E

1 mark

Have a go

1 Which image is a view of the 3D solid on the left from the direction of the arrow? Circle the correct letter.

1 mark

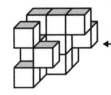 ←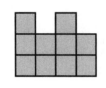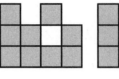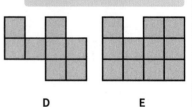

A B C D E

2 Which image is a view of the 3D solid on the left from the direction of the arrow? Circle the correct letter.

1 mark

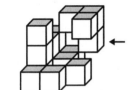 ←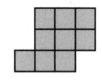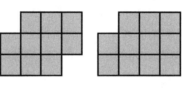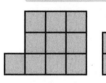

A B C D E

3 Which image is a view of the 3D solid on the left from the direction of the arrow? Circle the correct letter.

1 mark

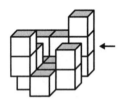 ←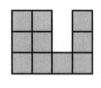

A B C D E

4 Which image is a view of the 3D solid on the left from the direction of the arrow? Circle the correct letter.

1 mark

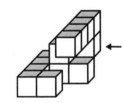 ←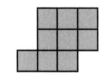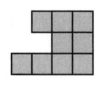

A B C D E

Time to reflect

Mark your *Have a go* section out of 4. How are you doing so far?

Check your answers in the back of the book and see how you are doing.

Had a go
0–2 marks

Nearly there
2–3 marks

Nailed it!
4 marks

Have another look at the *Worked example* on page 50. Then try these questions again.

Look at your incorrect answers. Make sure you understand how to get the correct answer.

Congratulations! Now see whether you can get full marks on the *Timed practice*.

When you are ready, try the *Timed practice* on the next page.

Timed practice

4

1 Which image is a view of the 3D solid on the left from the direction of the arrow? Circle the correct letter.

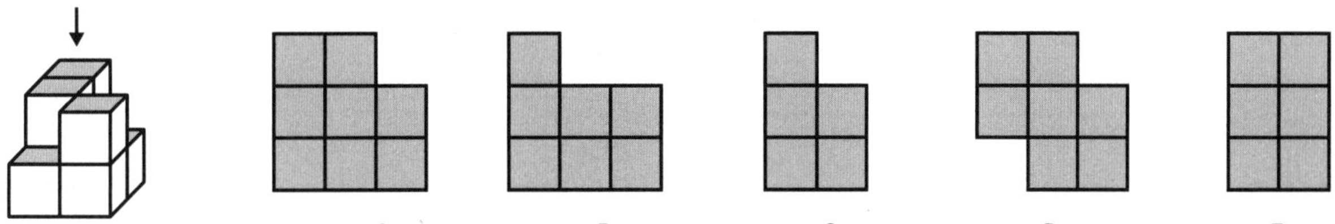

A   B   C   D   E

1 mark

2 Which image is a view of the 3D solid on the left from the direction of the arrow? Circle the correct letter.

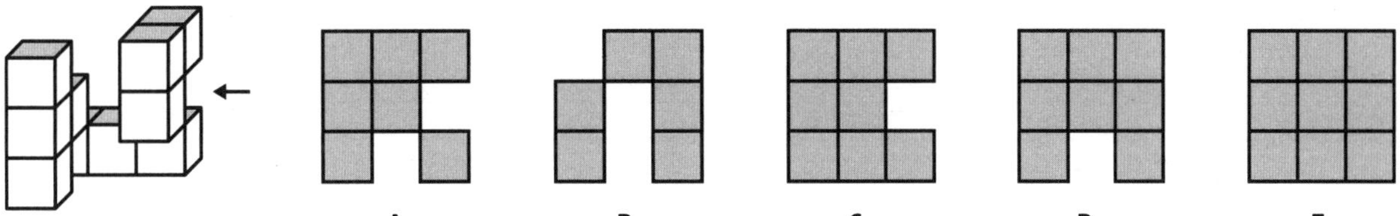

A   B   C   D   E

1 mark

3 Which image is a view of the 3D solid on the left from the direction of the arrow? Circle the correct letter.

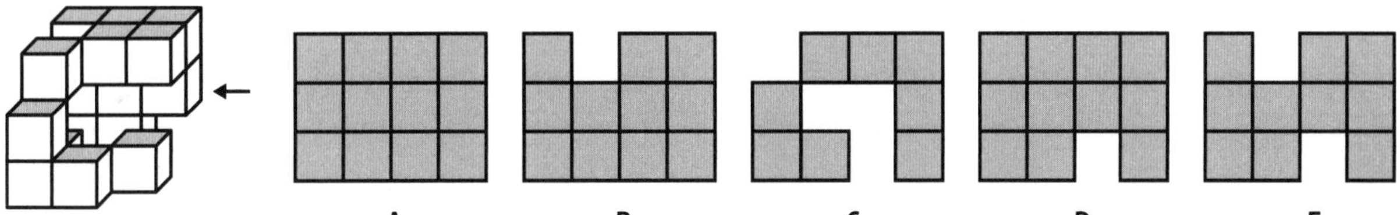

A   B   C   D   E

1 mark

4 Which image is a view of the 3D solid on the left from the direction of the arrow? Circle the correct letter.

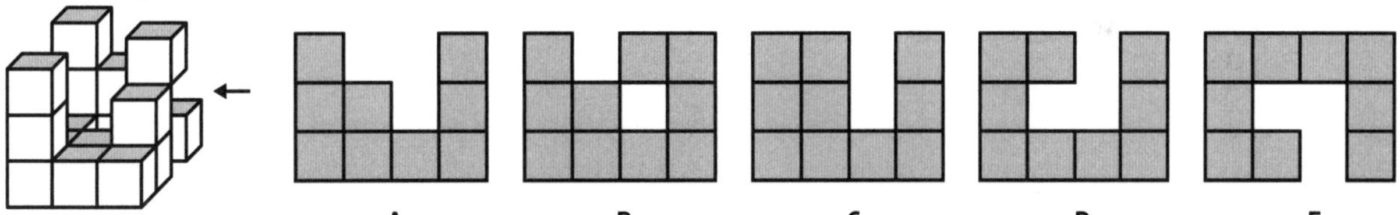

A   B   C   D   E

1 mark

5 Which image is a view of the 3D solid on the left from the direction of the arrow? Circle the correct letter.

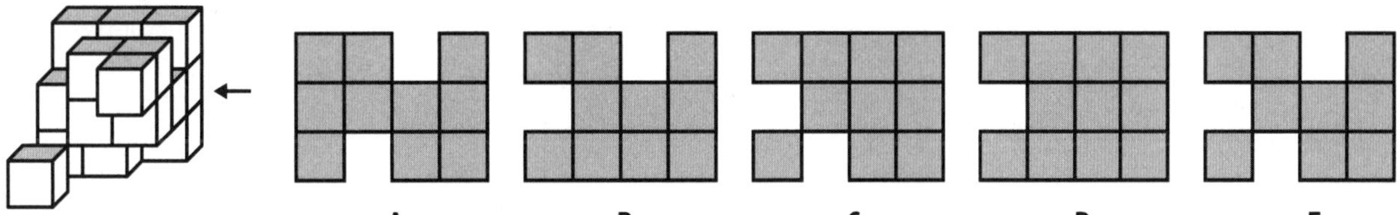

A   B   C   D   E

1 mark

Time to reflect

Mark your *Timed practice* section out of 5. How did you do?

Check your answers in the back of the book and write your score in the progress chart.

	0–3 marks
	Scan the QR code for extra practice.

Then move on to the next practice section or
try Test 23 in your Ten-Minute Tests book.

	4–5 marks
	Well done!

Move on to the next practice section or try
Test 23 in your Ten-Minute Tests book.

11 3D rotation

Each question shows one of the 3D solids at the top of the page from a different angle. For each question, work out which of the 3D solids at the top is shown.

Worked examples

Look at these 3D solids.

The solids are all made out of cubes and cuboids.

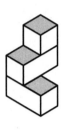

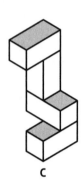

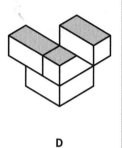

A   B   C   D

1 Which of the 3D solids at the top of the page has been rotated to make this view? Circle the correct letter.

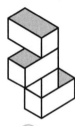

1 Imagine splitting each solid into cubes. This solid would be four cubes high, so C is too tall.

2 The 3D solid contains four shapes in a row. A only has two shapes in a row and D only has three shapes in a row.

3 The answer must be B.

A (B) C D

2 Which of the 3D solids at the top of the page has been rotated to make this view? Circle the correct letter.

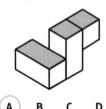

1 This solid is made out of two cuboids and one cube. It is three cubes long. Look at how long the 3D solids at the top of the page are in each direction. If any of them is longer than three cubes in any direction, then it is wrong.

2 B, C and D are all longer than three cubes, so the answer must be A.

(A) B C D

3 Which of the 3D solids at the top of the page has been rotated to make this view? Circle the correct letter.

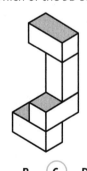

1 This 3D solid has four shapes stacked on top of each other. Compare it with the solids at the top of the page.

2 A only has three stacked shapes. D has four shapes, but they are not stacked on top of each other.

3 B has four stacked shapes but is only four cubes high. It is too short to be the answer.

4 C is five cubes high and has four shapes stacked on top of each other, so it matches this solid.

A B (C) D

Beyond the exam

Use building blocks or toy bricks to build a 3D solid made out of cubes and cuboids. Try turning your solid to see it from different angles. See if you can find an angle where one of the blocks is hidden, or where it looks like it could be a completely different shape.

Guided questions

Look at these 3D solids.

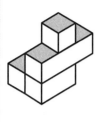

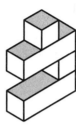

A   B   C   D   E

1 Which of the 3D solids at the top of the page has been rotated to make this view? Circle the correct letter.

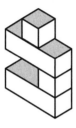

A   B   C   D   E

1 Look at how the shapes in the options are arranged. See if any of them match the solid in the question.

2 This solid has only been rotated 90°. Try solving the question by choosing the option that looks most similar.

123 Parallel means that two or more shapes or lines are next to each other and always the same distance apart. **Perpendicular** means that two shapes or lines are at a right angle to each other. Think about whether the cuboids in the solids above are parallel or perpendicular to each other.

2 Which of the 3D solids at the top of the page has been rotated to make this view? Circle the correct letter.

A   B   C   D   E

1 The cuboid in the middle of this solid touches all three of the other shapes.

2 Look at the options and cross out any that do not have this feature.

3 Which of the 3D solids at the top of the page has been rotated to make this view? Circle the correct letter.

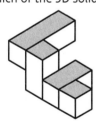

A   B   C   D   E

1 Look at the shapes that make each option and compare them to the view in the question. D has a T shape that cannot be right.

2 This 3D solid is made of one long cuboid, two shorter cuboids and a cube. Find the option that has the same shapes.

4 Which of the 3D solids at the top of the page has been rotated to make this view? Circle the correct letter.

A   B   C   D   E

This solid is made of at least four 3D shapes, but there might be others at the back that you cannot see.

Have a go

Look at these 3D solids.

  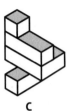 

A　　**B**　　**C**　　**D**　　**E**

 1 Which of the 3D solids at the top of the page has been rotated to make this view? Circle the correct letter.

1
mark

A　B　C　D　E

> Cross out any options that have too many parts, or whose parts are the wrong shape. However, remember that there might be shapes you cannot see.

2 Which of the 3D solids at the top of the page has been rotated to make this view? Circle the correct letter.

1
mark

A　B　C　D　E

> If there are shapes in a row in the rotated solid, they must also be in a row in the correct solid at the top of the page.

3 Which of the 3D solids at the top of the page has been rotated to make this view? Circle the correct letter.

1
mark

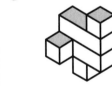

A　B　C　D　E

> If you think you know which is the right option, try rotating it in your head and see if you can make it match the view in the question.

4 Which of the 3D solids at the top of the page has been rotated to make this view? Circle the correct letter.

1
mark

A　B　C　D　E

> Remember, you might not be able to see the whole of each shape that makes up the 3D solid.

Time to reflect

Mark your *Have a go* section out of 4. How are you doing so far?

Check your answers in the back of the book and see how you are doing.

☐ **Had a go**
0–1 marks

☐ **Nearly there**
2–3 marks

☐ **Nailed it!**
4 marks

Have another look at the *Worked example* on page 54. Then try these questions again.

Look at your incorrect answers. Make sure you understand how to get the correct answer.

Congratulations! Now see whether you can get full marks on the *Timed practice*.

When you are ready, try the *Timed practice* on the next page.

Timed practice

Look at these 3D solids.

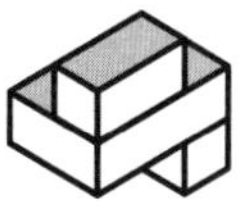

A 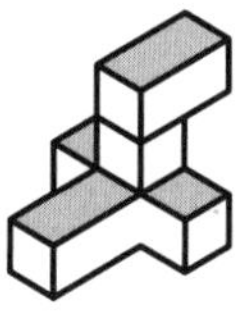   **B** 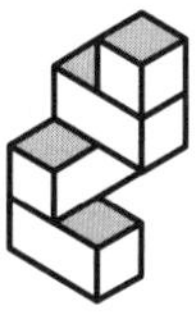   **C**    **D**    **E**

1 Which of the 3D solids at the top of the page has been rotated to make this view? Circle the correct letter.

      A   B   C   D   E

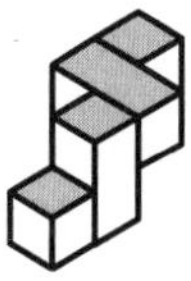

1 mark

2 Which of the 3D solids at the top of the page has been rotated to make this view? Circle the correct letter.

      A   B   C   D   E

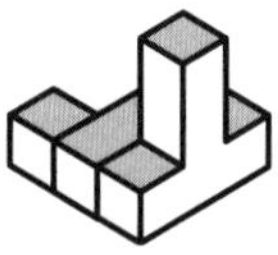

1 mark

3 Which of the 3D solids at the top of the page has been rotated to make this view? Circle the correct letter.

      A   B   C   D   E

1 mark

4 Which of the 3D solids at the top of the page has been rotated to make this view? Circle the correct letter.

      A   B   C   D   E

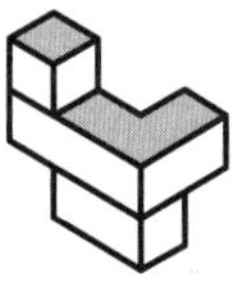

1 mark

5 Which of the 3D solids at the top of the page has been rotated to make this view? Circle the correct letter.

      A   B   C   D   E

1 mark

Time to reflect

Mark your *Timed practice* section out of 5. How did you do?

Check your answers in the back of the book and write your score in the progress chart.

☐ *0–3 marks*
    Scan the QR code for extra practice.
Then move on to the next practice section or
try Test 24 in your Ten-Minute Tests book.

☐ *4–5 marks*
    Well done!
Move on to the next practice section or try
Test 24 in your Ten-Minute Tests book.

12 Different views of 3D solids

Each of these questions shows a 3D solid with an arrow. You need to work out which image shows what the solid would look like when viewed from the direction of the arrow.

Worked example

1 Which view shows the 3D solid on the left from the direction of the arrow? Circle the correct letter.

> You can see three cuboids here, so you know that the solid is made up of at least three simple shapes. There could be others that are hidden from view.

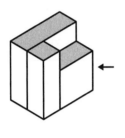  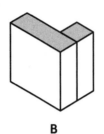 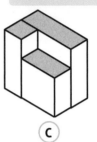 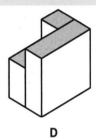

A   B   C   D

1 When viewed from the right, the three shapes will all still be visible because none of them is hidden by another shape. You can only see two shapes in B, so it is wrong.

2 The cuboids in A are at the right angle, but have changed shape. This solid is not long enough.

3 If viewed from the right, the shorter cuboid would be closer to you than the others. D shows the wrong angle, so the answer is C.

Guided questions

1 Which view shows the 3D solid on the left from the direction of the arrow? Circle the correct letter.

> This 3D solid is constructed from at least three shapes. These shapes must be the same in the correct view.

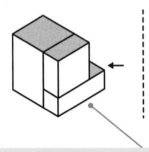 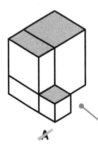 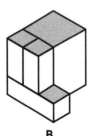 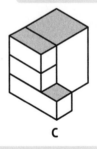 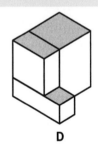

A   B   C   D

> The right face consists of two shapes. When viewed from the right, these will become the left face.

> Cross out any options with more than two shapes visible on the left face.

2 Which view shows the 3D solid on the left from the direction of the arrow? Circle the correct letter.

> The arrow in this question points down, so the view must show the 3D solid from above. Remember that the views are still 3D, so you will be able to see the sides of the shapes.

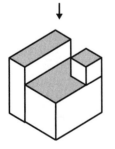 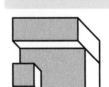 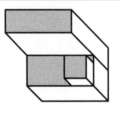 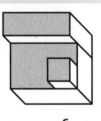 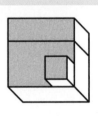

A   B   C   D

1 The cube is on the right in the image showing the 3D solid. It will still be on the right when viewed from above.

2 The top of the cube and the top of the cuboid at the back are at the same height. They will still look the same height when viewed from above.

Guided question

1 Which view shows the 3D solid on the left from the direction of the arrow? Circle the correct letter.

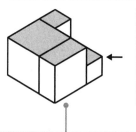 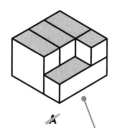 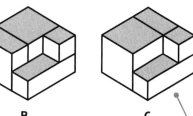

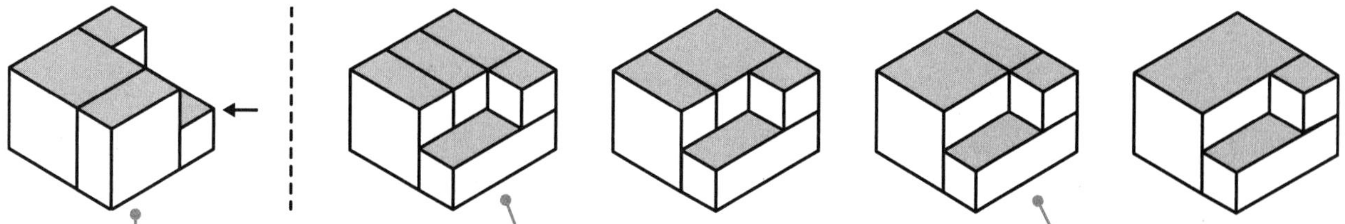

A   B   C   D

You can see three shapes
at the top of this 3D solid:
a large square, a small
square and a rectangle.

A has more than three
shapes on the top layer, so
it must be wrong.

The top layer of the correct view will have
a large grey square in between a smaller
square and a rectangle. Use this to decide
which is the correct answer.

Have a go

1 Which view shows the 3D solid on the left from the direction of the arrow? Circle the correct letter.

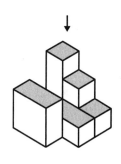 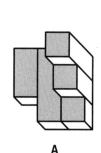 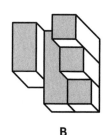 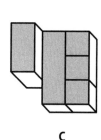 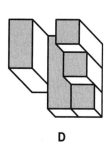

A   B   C   D

1 mark

You know the tallest shapes in the 3D solid will definitely be visible when
the solid is viewed from above, so start with these. Check that they have the
right height and position in each view.

2 Which view shows the 3D solid on the left from the direction of the arrow? Circle the correct letter.

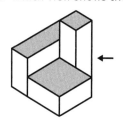 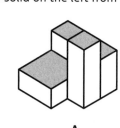 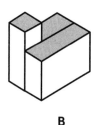 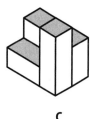 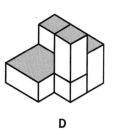

A   B   C   D

1 mark

Always think carefully about which
direction the arrow is pointing in.

Beyond the exam

Use a net to make a 3D model of a building. Draw features on it such as windows and doors. Pick one feature and then
slowly rotate the building, imagining you are walking around it. Work out how far you could walk in each direction
until you wouldn't be able to see the feature.

Have a go

1 Which view shows the 3D solid on the left from the direction of the arrow? Circle the correct letter.

Work out which shapes in the 3D solid would be visible from the right and check whether they are shown in each view.

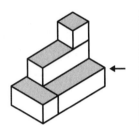 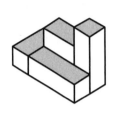 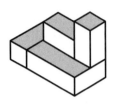  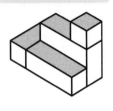

A   B   C   D

1 mark

2 Which view shows the 3D solid on the left from the direction of the arrow? Circle the correct letter.

Compare the heights of the shapes in the 3D solid. Check whether they are the right height in each view.

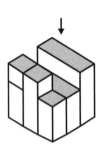 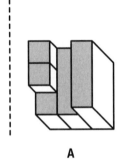 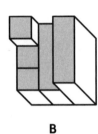 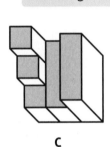 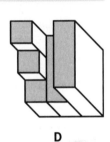

A   B   C   D

1 mark

3 Which view shows the 3D solid on the left from the direction of the arrow? Circle the correct letter.

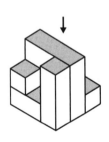 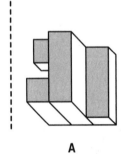 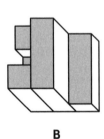 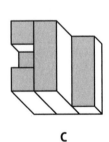 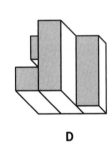

A   B   C   D

1 mark

In top-down views, you can work out the height of the shapes in the 3D solid from how much of their sides you can see. You could also think about how much of each shape is visible compared to those around it.

Time to reflect

Mark your *Have a go* section out of 3. How are you doing so far?

Check your answers in the back of the book and see how you are doing.

Had a go	**Nearly there**	**Nailed it!**
0–1 marks	*2 marks*	*3 marks*
Have another look at the *Worked example* on page 58. Then try these questions again.	Look at your incorrect answers. Make sure you understand how to get the correct answer.	Congratulations! Now see whether you can get full marks on the *Timed practice*.

When you are ready, try the *Timed practice* on the next page.

Timed practice

3

1 Which view shows the 3D solid on the left from the direction of the arrow? Circle the correct letter.

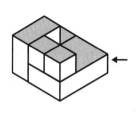 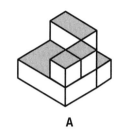 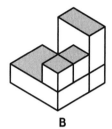 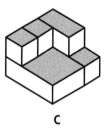 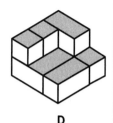

    A   B   C   D

1 mark

2 Which view shows the 3D solid on the left from the direction of the arrow? Circle the correct letter.

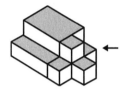 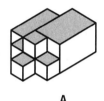 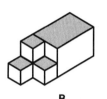 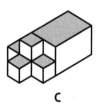 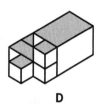

    A   B   C   D

1 mark

3 Which view shows the 3D solid on the left from the direction of the arrow? Circle the correct letter.

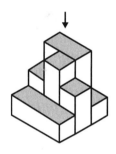 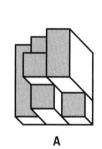 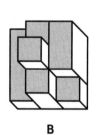 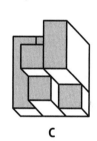 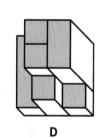

    A   B   C   D

1 mark

4 Which view shows the 3D solid on the left from the direction of the arrow? Circle the correct letter.

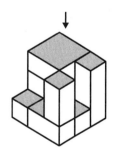 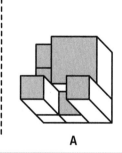 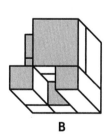 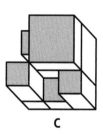 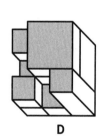

    A   B   C   D

1 mark

Time to reflect

Mark your *Timed practice* section out of 4. How did you do?
Check your answers in the back of the book and write your score in the progress chart.

☐ *0–2 marks*
  Scan the QR code for extra practice.
Then move on to the next practice section or
try Test 25 in your Ten-Minute Tests book.

☐ *3–4 marks*
  Well done!
Move on to the next practice section or try
Test 25 in your Ten-Minute Tests book.

13 Build the 3D solid

The 3D solid on the left in each of these questions has been built using one of the sets of 3D blocks on the right. Find the set of blocks that will make the 3D solid.

1 Which set of blocks builds the 3D solid on the left? Circle the correct letter.

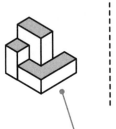 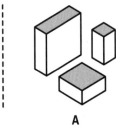 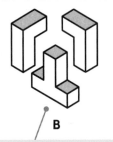 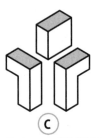 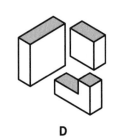

           A   **B**   **C**   **D**

You can see that this 3D solid is made of at least three blocks. Remember that you might not be able to see all of the blocks from this angle.

Each option has a different set of blocks. Only one set can make the 3D solid on the left.

The grey shading tells you where the top of each shape is. The same face might not be shaded in the 3D solid.

1 A and D both contain a large cuboid. This would not fit in the 3D solid on the left.

2 B contains a T shape that would not fit in the 3D solid.

3 The answer must be C. The cuboid is on the left, the end of one of the L shaped solids is on top, and the other L shape is on its side at the front.

1 Which set of blocks builds the 3D solid on the left? Circle the correct letter.

Use this cube to measure the sizes of the other blocks. The long cuboid in this set is three cubes high. The short cuboid in C is two cubes high.

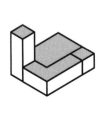 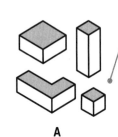 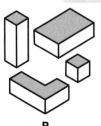 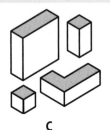 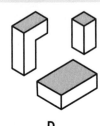

           A   **B**   **C**   **D**

1 There is a wide cuboid at the back of the 3D solid. This shape is only in sets B and D. Cross out A and C.

2 The long thin cuboid in the 3D solid is three cubes tall.

2 Which set of blocks builds the 3D solid on the left? Circle the correct letter.

Imagine fitting the blocks together in different ways.

 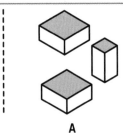 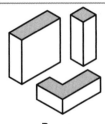 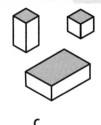 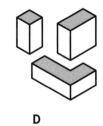

           A   **B**   **C**   **D**

1 The visible shape on the bottom layer must be either an L shape or a cuboid that is three cubes long and two cubes wide.

2 Imagine that it is a cuboid and work out what other shapes you would need to make the 3D solid. Then do the same for an L shape.

3 Look at the sets of blocks and find one that matches the blocks you worked out.

Guided questions

1 Which set of blocks builds the 3D solid on the left? Circle the correct letter.

> The back of this 3D solid is hidden, so you need to use the options to work out the answer.

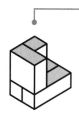 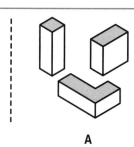 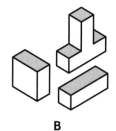 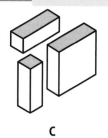 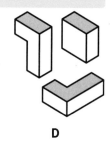

 A   B   C   D

1 One of the blocks is too large to fit in the 3D solid. Work out which it is and then cross out that option.

2 Look at the other options. One of them will leave a space where you can see part of a shape in the 3D solid.

3 Imagine fitting the blocks together to decide which of the last two options makes the 3D solid.

Have a go

1 Which set of blocks builds the 3D solid on the left? Circle the correct letter.

> Look carefully to see how many blocks the 3D solid is made from.

 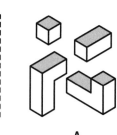 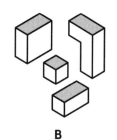 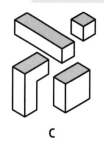 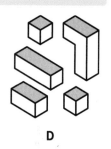

 A   B   C   D

`1` mark

2 Which set of blocks builds the 3D solid on the left? Circle the correct letter.

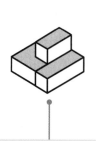 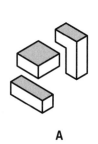  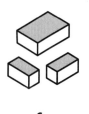 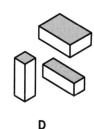

 A   B   C   D

`1` mark

> Imagine splitting the 3D solid into small cubes and count how many it contains. Use this to decide if any options do not have large enough blocks.

Beyond the exam

Draw an object you can see, such as a chair or table, and split it into cubes and cuboids. Cut out your shapes and mix them up. Then, see if you can put them back together correctly.

Have a go

1   Which set of blocks builds the 3D solid on the left? Circle the correct letter.

> For complex questions, try crossing out the wrong answers until you just have one left. Look at the shapes in each set and decide where one of them could fit. See if there would be room for the other blocks too.

 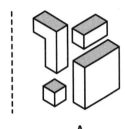 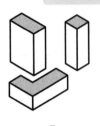  

A   B   C   D

1 mark

2   Which set of blocks builds the 3D solid on the left? Circle the correct letter.

> If you can see any whole shapes in the 3D solid, start by crossing out any options that do not include those shapes.

 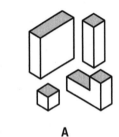   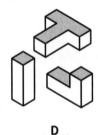

A   B   C   D

1 mark

3   Which set of blocks builds the 3D solid on the left? Circle the correct letter.

> Imagine building up from the base of the 3D solid, rather than down from the top. Fill in the shapes you know on each layer.

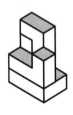 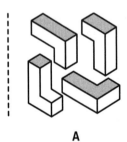  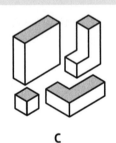 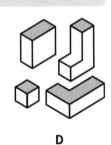

A   B   C   D

1 mark

Time to reflect

Mark your *Have a go* section out of 3. How are you doing so far?

Check your answers in the back of the book and see how you are doing.

☐ **Had a go**	☐ **Nearly there**	☐ **Nailed it!**
0–1 marks	*2 marks*	*3 marks*
Have another look at the *Worked example* on page 62. Then try these questions again.	Look at your incorrect answers. Make sure you understand how to get the correct answer.	Congratulations! Now see whether you can get full marks on the *Timed practice*.

When you are ready, try the *Timed practice* on the next page.

Timed practice

③

1 Which set of blocks builds the 3D solid on the left? Circle the correct letter.

 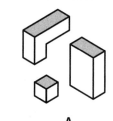 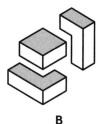 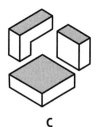 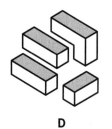

A   B   C   D

1 mark

2 Which set of blocks builds the 3D solid on the left? Circle the correct letter.

 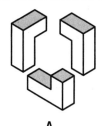 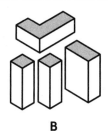 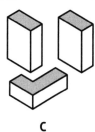 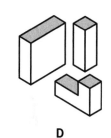

A   B   C   D

1 mark

3 Which set of blocks builds the 3D solid on the left? Circle the correct letter.

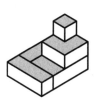 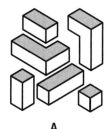 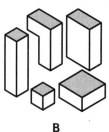 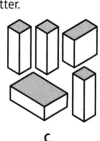 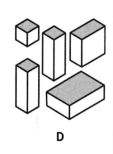

A   B   C   D

1 mark

4 Which set of blocks builds the 3D solid on the left? Circle the correct letter.

 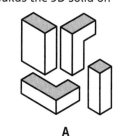 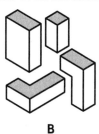 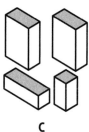 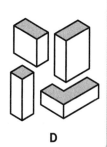

A   B   C   D

1 mark

Time to reflect

Mark your *Timed practice* section out of 4. How did you do?

Check your answers in the back of the book and write your score in the progress chart.

▢ *0–2 marks*
Scan the QR code for extra practice.
Then move on to the next practice section or
try Test 26 in your Ten-Minute Tests book.

▢ *3–4 marks*
Well done!
Move on to the next practice section or try
Test 26 in your Ten-Minute Tests book.

14 Fold and punch

Imagine folding a square of paper and then punching holes in it. In each of these questions, work out what the paper on the left would look like when it was unfolded.

Worked example

1 This piece of paper has been folded and holes have been punched out of it. Which image will the paper look like when it is unfolded? Circle the correct letter.

The arrows show you how the paper has been folded. This piece has been folded once horizontally and once vertically to make a small square.

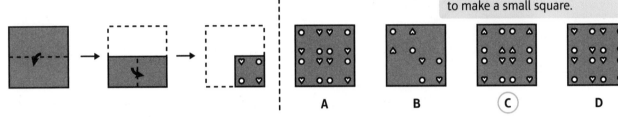

A   B   C   D

1 The paper has been folded in half twice, making four layers. This means that each of the four punched holes has gone through the paper four times. 4 × 4 = 16, so you are looking for an answer with 16 holes. B is wrong.

2 Each fold acts as a line of symmetry. The first fold is horizontal, so there must be a horizontal line of symmetry across the middle of the unfolded paper. A and D are both wrong.

3 The second fold means that the paper has a vertical line of symmetry. Check that C is the right answer by making sure it has a vertical line of symmetry.

Guided questions

1 This piece of paper has been folded and holes have been punched out of it. Which image will the paper look like when it is unfolded? Circle the correct letter.

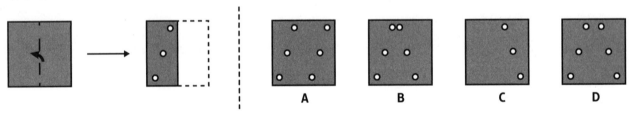

A   B   C   D

1 This paper is folded once, so each hole has punched through two layers of paper. There will be six holes in the unfolded paper.

2 The paper was folded exactly in half, so the unfolded paper should have a vertical line of symmetry down the middle.

2 This piece of paper has been folded and holes have been punched out of it. Which image will the paper look like when it is unfolded? Circle the correct letter.

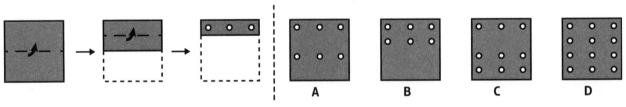

A   B   C   D

1 Think about how many layers of paper each hole has punched through. Use this to work out how many holes there should be when the paper is unfolded.

2 Check which options have the right number of holes.

Beyond the exam

Fold some square pieces of paper and use a hole punch to make some holes in them. Experiment to work out where you need to punch the holes to make a pattern, such as a star or a flower.

Guided questions

1 This piece of paper has been folded and a hole has been punched out of it.
Which image will the paper look like when it is unfolded? Circle the correct letter.

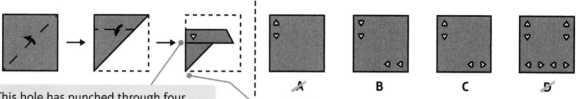

A   B   C   D

This hole has punched through four layers of paper. So the unfolded paper must have four holes. Cross out A and D.

The second fold doesn't reach all the way down, so a hole in this section would only punch through two layers of paper.

2 This piece of paper has been folded and holes have been punched out of it. Which image will the paper look like when it is unfolded? Circle the correct letter.

The third fold stacks the first two folds on top of each other. Any holes punched in the middle section of the paper would punch through four layers of paper.

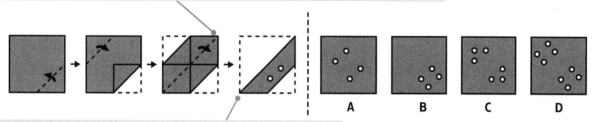

A   B   C   D

A hole at either end would only go through two layers of paper.

3 This piece of paper has been folded and holes have been punched out of it. Which image will the paper look like when it is unfolded? Circle the correct letter.

If a hole is punched on a part of the paper that has not been folded, it will only go through one layer. So it will only make one hole.

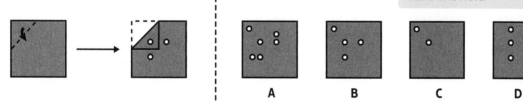

A   B   C   D

Have a go

1 This piece of paper has been folded and holes have been punched out of it. Which image will the paper look like when it is unfolded? Circle the correct letter.

Try drawing the holes on the final fold diagram. Start with the holes you would expect after undoing the last fold. Then repeat with the remaining folds, working back to the first one.

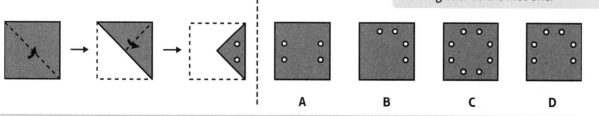

A   B   C   D

1 mark

Have a go

1 This piece of paper has been folded and a hole has been punched out of it. Which image will the paper look like when it is unfolded? Circle the correct letter.

> Count how many times the part of the paper with the hole has been folded.

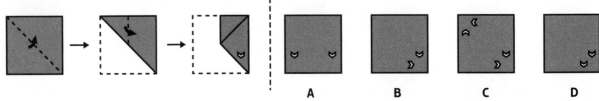

A   B   C   D

1 mark

2 This piece of paper has been folded and holes have been punched out of it. Which image will the paper look like when it is unfolded? Circle the correct letter.

> Try drawing the folds onto the images on the right. Use them as lines of symmetry to help you work out where each hole should be.

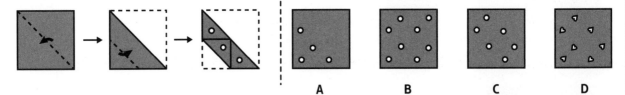

A   B   C   D

1 mark

3 This piece of paper has been folded and holes have been punched out of it. Which image will the paper look like when it is unfolded? Circle the correct letter.

> Start by working out how many holes there should be.

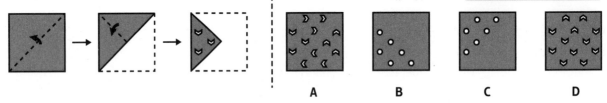

A   B   C   D

1 mark

4 This piece of paper has been folded and a hole has been punched out of it. Which image will the paper look like when it is unfolded? Circle the correct letter.

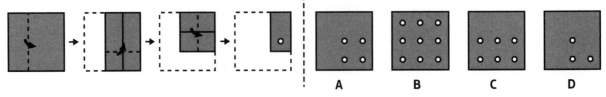

A   B   C   D

1 mark

Time to reflect

Mark your *Have a go* section out of 4. How are you doing so far?

Check your answers in the back of the book and see how you are doing.

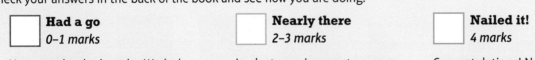

Had a go 0–1 marks	**Nearly there** 2–3 marks	**Nailed it!** 4 marks
Have another look at the *Worked example* on page 66. Then try these questions again.	Look at your incorrect answers. Make sure you understand how to get the correct answer.	Congratulations! Now see whether you can get full marks on the *Timed practice*.

When you are ready, try the *Timed practice* on the next page.

Timed practice

🕐 **4**

1 This piece of paper has been folded and holes have been punched out of it. Which image will the paper look like when it is unfolded? Circle the correct letter.

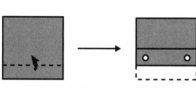 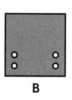

                        A   B   C   D

`1` mark

2 This piece of paper has been folded and holes have been punched out of it. Which image will the paper look like when it is unfolded? Circle the correct letter.

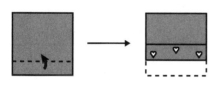

                        A   B   C   D

`1` mark

3 This piece of paper has been folded and holes have been punched out of it. Which image will the paper look like when it is unfolded? Circle the correct letter.

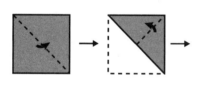

                        A   B   C   D

`1` mark

4 This piece of paper has been folded and holes have been punched out of it. Which image will the paper look like when it is unfolded? Circle the correct letter.

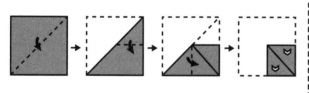

                        A   B   C   D

`1` mark

5 This piece of paper has been folded and a hole has been punched out of it. Which image will the paper look like when it is unfolded? Circle the correct letter.

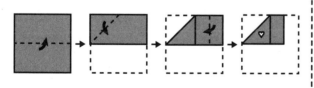

                        A   B   C   D

`1` mark

Time to reflect

Mark your *Timed practice* section out of 5. How did you do?

Check your answers in the back of the book and write your score in the progress chart.

☐ *0–3 marks*
    Scan the QR code for extra practice.
Then try the *Progress test* or try Test 28 in
your Ten-Minute Tests book.

☐ *4–5 marks*
    Well done!
Try the *Progress test* or try Test 28 in your
Ten-Minute Tests book.

Progress test

Complete this test once you have worked through all the practice sections in this book. It covers all the topics in this book and is as hard as a real 11+ test.

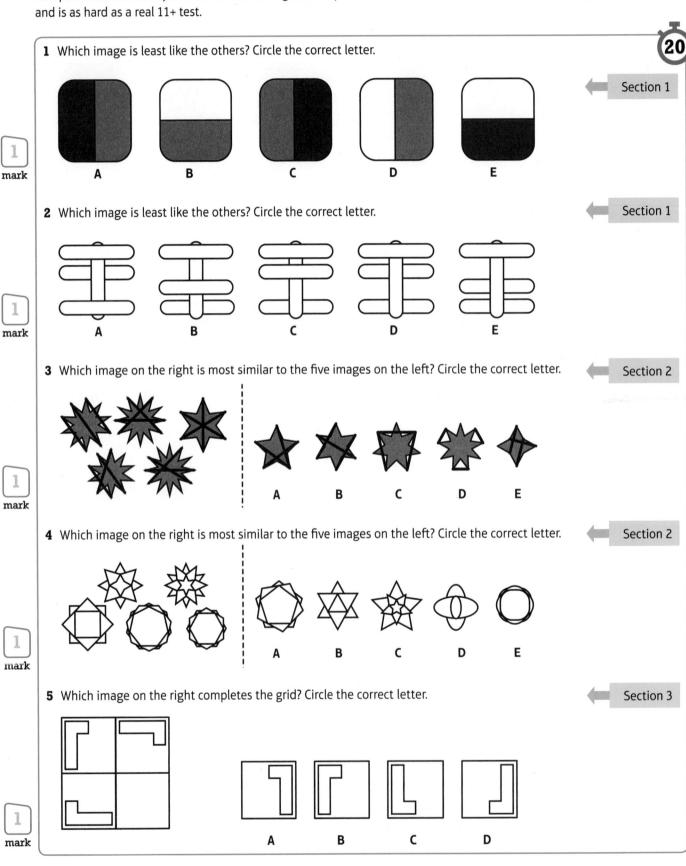

1 Which image is least like the others? Circle the correct letter.

A   B   C   D   E

Section 1

1 mark

2 Which image is least like the others? Circle the correct letter.

A   B   C   D   E

Section 1

1 mark

3 Which image on the right is most similar to the five images on the left? Circle the correct letter.

A   B   C   D   E

Section 2

1 mark

4 Which image on the right is most similar to the five images on the left? Circle the correct letter.

A   B   C   D   E

Section 2

1 mark

5 Which image on the right completes the grid? Circle the correct letter.

A   B   C   D

Section 3

1 mark

6 Which image on the right completes the grid? Circle the correct letter.

Section 3

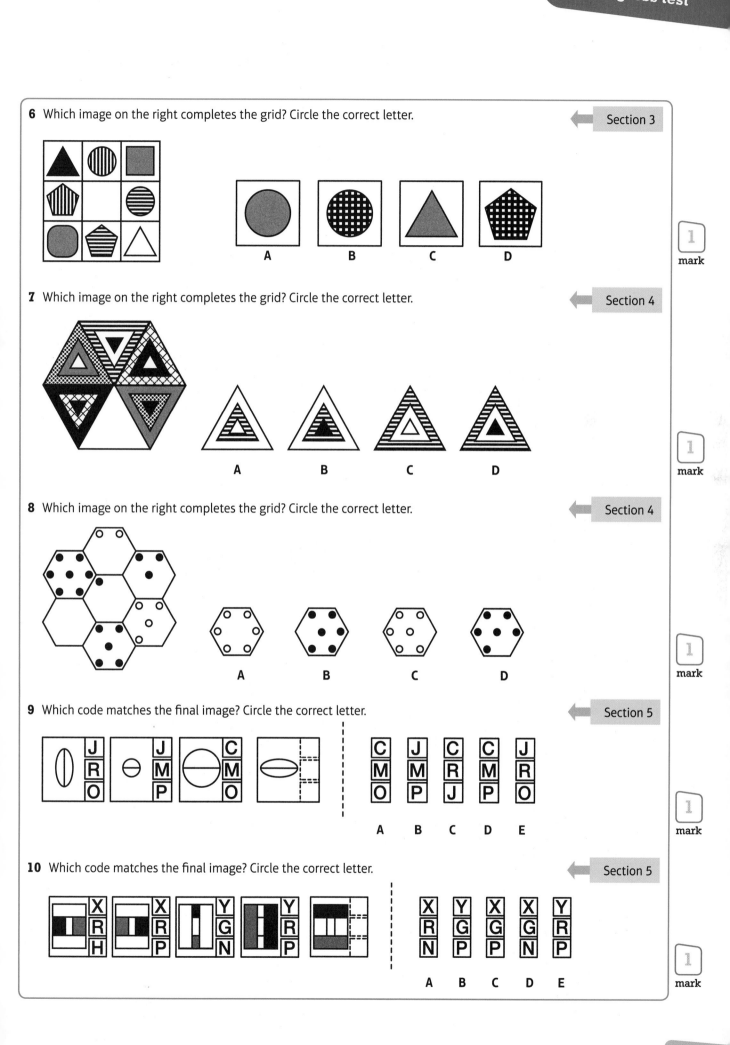

1 mark

7 Which image on the right completes the grid? Circle the correct letter.

Section 4

1 mark

8 Which image on the right completes the grid? Circle the correct letter.

Section 4

1 mark

9 Which code matches the final image? Circle the correct letter.

Section 5

1 mark

10 Which code matches the final image? Circle the correct letter.

Section 5

1 mark

11 Which code matches the final image? Circle the correct letter.

Section 6

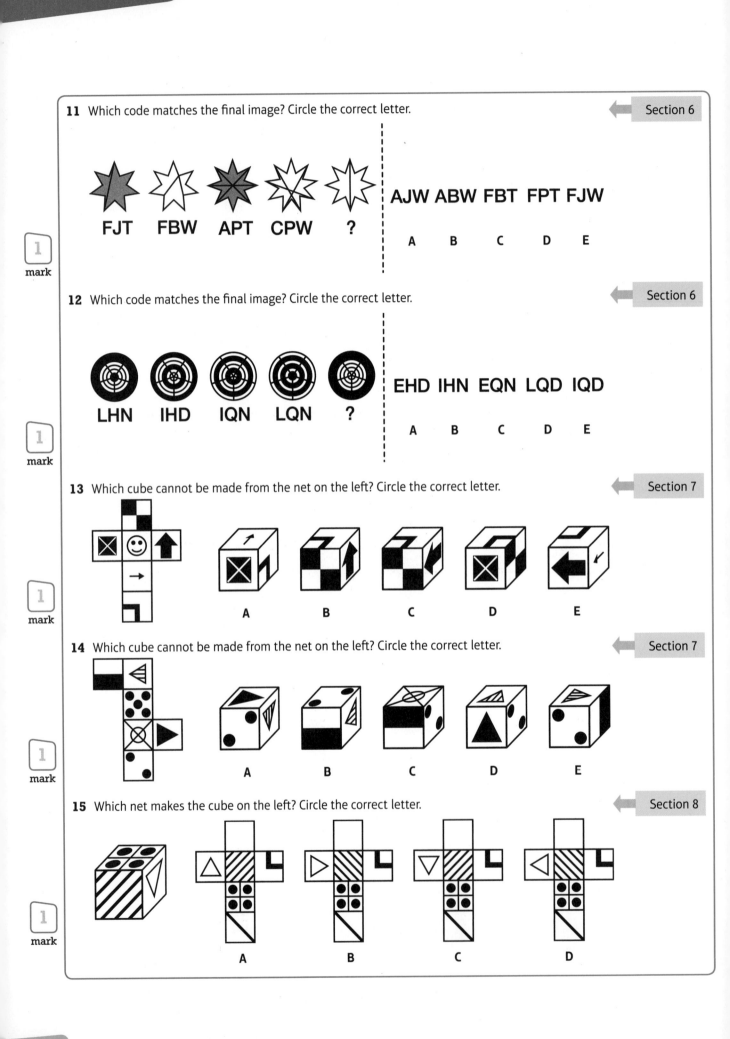

FJT   FBW   APT   CPW   ?

AJW   ABW   FBT   FPT   FJW

A   B   C   D   E

1 mark

12 Which code matches the final image? Circle the correct letter.

Section 6

LHN   IHD   IQN   LQN   ?

EHD   IHN   EQN   LQD   IQD

A   B   C   D   E

1 mark

13 Which cube cannot be made from the net on the left? Circle the correct letter.

Section 7

A   B   C   D   E

1 mark

14 Which cube cannot be made from the net on the left? Circle the correct letter.

Section 7

A   B   C   D   E

1 mark

15 Which net makes the cube on the left? Circle the correct letter.

Section 8

A   B   C   D

1 mark

16 Which net makes the cube on the left? Circle the correct letter. ← Section 8

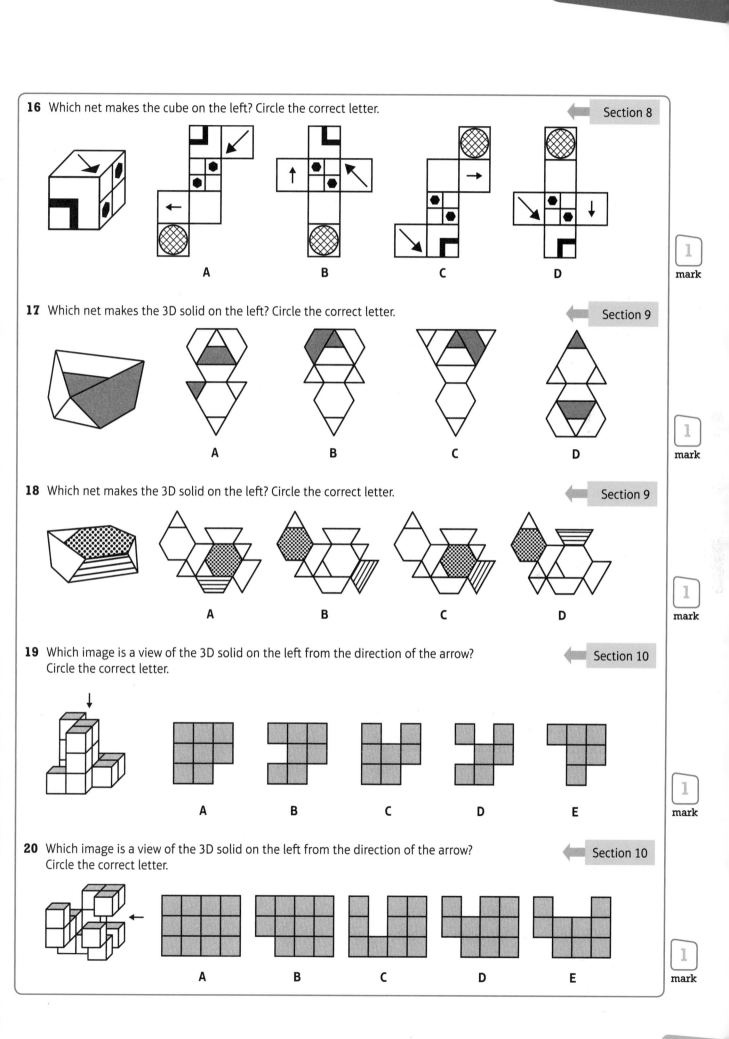

A   B   C   D

1 mark

17 Which net makes the 3D solid on the left? Circle the correct letter. ← Section 9

A   B   C   D

1 mark

18 Which net makes the 3D solid on the left? Circle the correct letter. ← Section 9

A   B   C   D

1 mark

19 Which image is a view of the 3D solid on the left from the direction of the arrow? Circle the correct letter. ← Section 10

A   B   C   D   E

1 mark

20 Which image is a view of the 3D solid on the left from the direction of the arrow? Circle the correct letter. ← Section 10

A   B   C   D   E

1 mark

Look at these 3D solids.

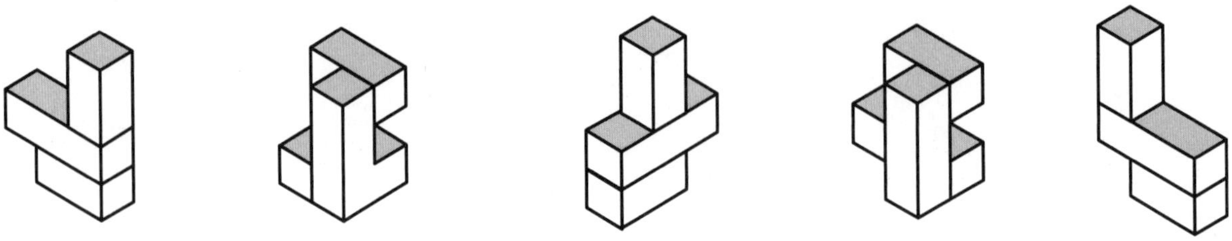

| A | B | C | D | E |

21 Which of the 3D solids at the top of the page has been rotated to make this view? Circle the correct letter.

Section 11

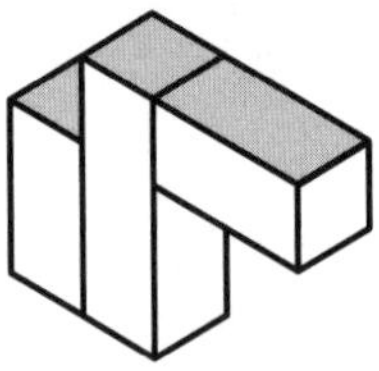

A   B   C   D   E

1 mark

22 Which of the 3D solids at the top of the page has been rotated to make this view? Circle the correct letter.

Section 11

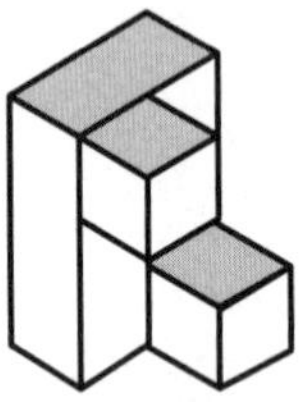

A   B   C   D   E

1 mark

23 Which view shows the 3D solid on the left from the direction of the arrow? Circle the correct letter.

Section 12

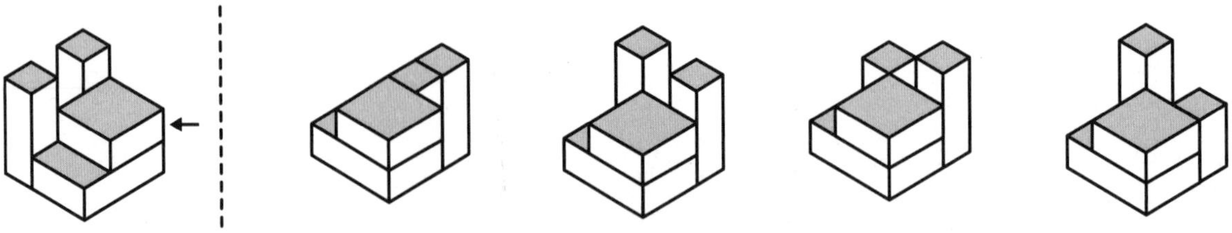

| A | B | C | D |

1 mark

24 Which view shows the 3D solid on the left from the direction of the arrow? Circle the correct letter.

Section 12

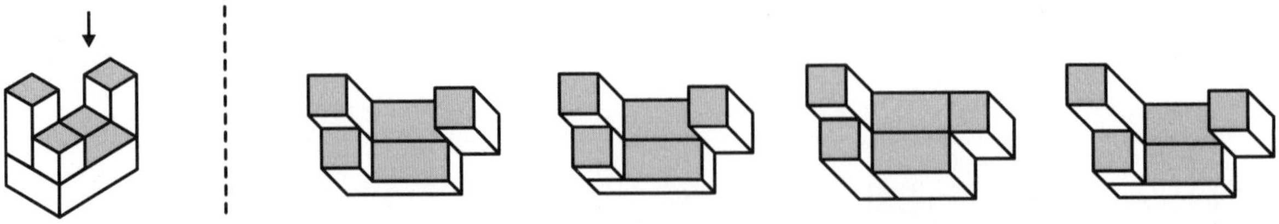

| A | B | C | D |

1 mark

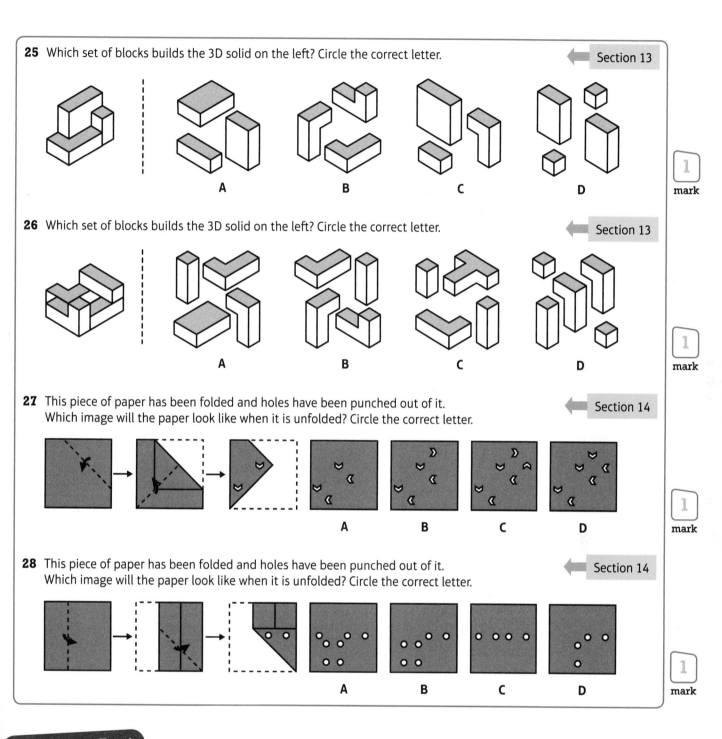

25 Which set of blocks builds the 3D solid on the left? Circle the correct letter.

Section 13

A   B   C   D

1 mark

26 Which set of blocks builds the 3D solid on the left? Circle the correct letter.

Section 13

A   B   C   D

1 mark

27 This piece of paper has been folded and holes have been punched out of it. Which image will the paper look like when it is unfolded? Circle the correct letter.

Section 14

A   B   C   D

1 mark

28 This piece of paper has been folded and holes have been punched out of it. Which image will the paper look like when it is unfolded? Circle the correct letter.

Section 14

A   B   C   D

1 mark

Time to reflect

Mark your *Progress test* out of 28. How did you do?

[ ] *0–22 marks*
Use the section links to identify your strengths and weaknesses. Revisit the practice sections you scored the lowest in and then scan the QR code to try more mixed questions.

[ ] *23–28 marks*
Use the section links to identify your strengths and weaknesses. You might want to revisit the practice sections you scored the lowest in.

Answers

Diagnostic test

Page 2

1 D:

The other images are all five-sided shapes.

2 B:

B is the only image that does not contain a black shape. It is also the only image in which the smallest square is grey.

3 C:

The images on the left both contain three regular polygons of the same size, colour and orientation. The middle polygon is in front of the other two polygons. The polygons line up.

4 C:

The images on the left all contain a four-pointed star and a curved shape.

5 A:

On each row, the image rotates 45° and the black and white colours swap.

Page 3

6 C:

In each column, the arrow grows in a different way. In the left column, the arrow gets longer. In the middle column, the arrowhead increases in size. In the right column, the line gets thicker.

7 D:

Starting from the missing piece and reading clockwise, the circles increase in size. Triangles opposite one another contain the same style of line.

8 B:

The hexagons around the edge have alternating patterns. The vertex of the large triangle is needed to complete the pattern. Each hexagon is the same colour as the one opposite it.

9 E: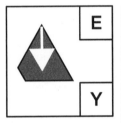

The first letter shows the direction of the arrow (M – up, E – down). The second letter shows which vertex of the triangle is missing (V – top, Y – left, K – right).

10 A:

The first letter shows the number of stars (A – one, B – two, O – three). The second letter shows the number of points on the stars (P – five, C – seven). The third letter shows the position of the black star (W – top, F – middle, T – bottom).

Page 4

11 E:

VI

The first letter shows the orientation of the inner shape (V – side at the top, M – vertex at the top). The second letter shows the colour of the outer shape (D – black, K – grey, I – white).

12 D: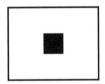

BAT

The first letter shows the inner shape (B – square, H – circle). The second letter shows the colour of the outer shape (A – white, U – black). The third letter shows how many sides the outer shape has (G – one, T – four).

13 B:

B and E are the same apart from their front face. B is wrong because the double-ended arrow is pointing in the wrong direction.

14 E:

On the top face, the white half of the circle should be next to the small grid on the front face.

15 B:

In A and C, the striped triangle would not have a flat side next to the hatched circle. In D, the line through the small circle is not pointing at the hatched circle.

Page 5

16 D: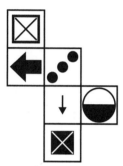

In A, the bold arrow does not point at the black square. In B, the small arrow does not point at the black square. In C, the two arrows do not share an edge so would be on opposite sides.

17 C:

In A, the grey rectangle is on the wrong side. B and D would not make a 3D solid.

18 C:

In A, the grey triangle pointing towards the rectangle should be white, and the top triangle should be grey. In B, the grey triangles would be on opposite sides of the 3D solid. In D, the grey triangle would be on the wrong side of the 3D solid.

19. C:

The correct answer must have two squares in the bottom row on the left, and two squares in the middle row on the right. It must also have three squares in the top row. B is the only image that matches this description.

20 E: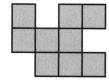

The correct answer must have two squares at the top in the first column, and two squares at the bottom in the second column. It must also have one square at the top and one at the bottom of the fourth column. E is the only image that matches this description.

Page 6

21 D: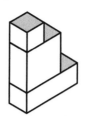

The 3D solid contains one cube. A, B and C do not have any cubes. E has two cubes.

22 A: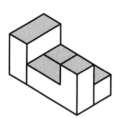

The 3D solid has an L shape with no other shape beneath the short side. C and D do not have an L shape. B and E have another shape next to the short side of the L shape.

23 A: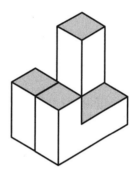

In B, the two shapes at the front are not the same height. In C, the cuboid at the back is too short. In D, there is an extra cube next to the cuboid at the back.

24 D: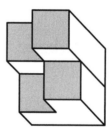

In A and B, the small L shape at the front has been split into two shapes. In C, the back left cuboid is too short.

Page 7

25 C: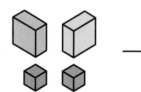

26 D: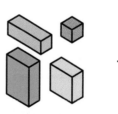

27 D: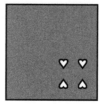

In A, the bottom hearts are upside down. In B, the holes are the wrong shape. C is missing two holes.

28 C:

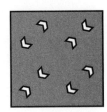

A is missing the top right hole. B is missing the top right and bottom left holes. In D, the holes are all pointing in the wrong direction.

1 Odd one out

Page 8 Guided questions

1 E:

In all the other images, the smaller rectangle is above the bigger one.

2 A:

The shapes in all the other images have the same number of sides as the number of dots.

Page 9 Guided questions

1 D:

All the other shapes have a square or rectangle in the middle.

2 B:

All the other images have two black squares and three white squares.

Page 9 Have a go

1 A:

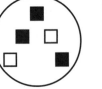

In all the other images, the dotted circle is opposite the dashed line.

2 D:

In all the other images, the inner shape and the outer shape have the same number of sides.

Page 10 Have a go

1 C:

All the other images are rotations, not reflections.

2 E:

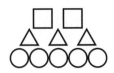

In all the other images, each row has one less shape than the row below it. In E, the middle row has two shapes less than the row below it.

3 D:

All the other images have the same number of black and white rectangles.

4 C:

In all the other images, the two arrows point in opposite directions.

Page 11 Timed practice

1 D:

In all the other images, the diagonal shading in the square goes in the opposite direction.

2 A:

All the other images contain an even number of shapes.

3 E:

In all the other images, the lines cross in five places. In E, the lines cross in six places.

4 B:

In all the other images, the rectangle overlaps to make the same shape.

5 B:

In all the other images, the shape outside the square is the same as the most common shape inside the square.

2 Which image belongs?

Page 12 Guided questions

1 B:

The images on the left all have five sides.

2 E:

The images on the left are all transparent cubes.

Page 13 Guided questions

1 C:

The images on the left all contain a curved line with one vertical oval, one horizontal oval and one diagonal oval.

2 C:

The images on the left all contain a six-sided shape with four shapes inside it.

Page 13 Have a go

1 A:

The images on the left all contain a line with four segments.

2 E:

The images on the left all contain three shapes. The shapes have the same orientation, but the line style alternates between dotted and solid.

Page 14 Have a go

1 B:

The images on the left all contain a black circle, a white star and an arrow pointing at the star.

2 E:

The images on the left all contain one black and one white shape of the same type. The smaller shape is in the corner of the bigger shape.

3 A:

The images on the left all contain an identical curved line with two arrows pointing at it.

4 C:

The images on the left all contain six shapes, three of which are the same type and size.

Page 15 Timed practice

1 C:

The images on the left all contain isosceles triangles.

2 D: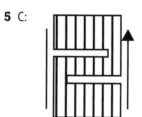

The images on the left all contain two shapes of the same type on either side of a different shape. They all have vertical and horizontal symmetry.

3 E:

The images on the left all contain only white circles and black ovals.

4 D: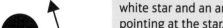

The images on the left all contain a circle with one quarter removed. The quarter circle is rotated 180° and appears in the image twice.

5 C:

The images on the left all contain a striped shape and an arrow pointing in the same direction as the stripes.

3 Complete the square grid

Page 16 Guided questions

1 B:

The stars in the top row are reflected vertically. The line changes from solid to dashed in the bottom row.

2 B:

The arrow rotates by 90° as you read clockwise around the grid.

Page 17 Guided questions

1 A:

Reading across, the number of sides increases by one. Reading down, the shape gets larger and lightens in colour.

2 A:

Each row has one five-pointed star, one six-pointed star and one seven-pointed star. On each row, one of the stars has a thin outline, one has a medium outline and one has a thick outline.

Page 17 Have a go

1 D:

Only D contains the missing sections of the black circle, the vertical thick black line and the diagonal thin black line.

Page 18 Have a go

1 C:

The grid has symmetry in a diagonal line from bottom left to top right, so the correct image completes the black circle and white square.

2 D:

Each row and column contain one black, one grey and one white circle. There is a solid line around the inside and a dashed line around the outside.

3 A:

In each column, the shapes are in the same order. The white shape changes each time.

Page 19 Timed practice

1 A:

Reading from left to right and top to bottom, the number of circles increases by one each square, and the black circle moves clockwise around each square.

2 C:

The arrows point in a clockwise spiral from the flat line in the middle square to the flat line in the top left square. Each arrow points at the tail of the next one.

3 B:

The pattern of the left shape in the middle column matches the pattern of the shape in the left column. The pattern of the right shape in the middle column matches the pattern of the shape in the right column.

4 D:

The completed grid has a vertical line of symmetry, so the correct image is a reflection of the square in the middle row of the left column.

4 Complete the hexagonal grid

Page 20 Guided questions

1 C:

Starting at the top left triangle and reading clockwise, each triangle adds one more white line and one more black line.

2 D:

The solid lines form a hexagon around the outer six shapes. The dashed lines form a loop around the outer six shapes.

Page 21 Guided questions

1 D:

Each triangle of the same orientation contains an arrow in the same position.

2 B:

Starting at the top left hexagon and reading clockwise, each hexagon adds one new shape. The colours alternate between black and white.

Page 21 Have a go

1 C:

Each triangle has the same pattern as the one opposite it. There is an extra line on the alternate triangles.

Page 22 Have a go

1 C:

Starting at the bottom right hexagon and reading clockwise, the points of the large star increase by one in each hexagon. There are six-pointed stars overlapping each triangle. There is a six-pointed star in the middle.

2 B:

Hexagons opposite each other are identical.

3 D:

Hexagons with grey and white backgrounds alternate and the shapes inside them form a pattern. Reading clockwise around the grid, each circle is the same colour as the shape in the hexagon before it.

Page 23 Timed practice

1 B:

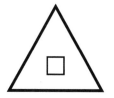

The squares in each row get larger from left to right.

2 A:

Triangles opposite each other contain the same shape. Reading clockwise around the hexagon, the dots are always on the right side of the triangle. The dots in the centre alternate between black and white.

3 A:

The pattern of each outer triangle matches the pattern of the inner triangle opposite it.

4 C:

Reading in a spiral up and clockwise from the centre, the triangle and oval point to the next hexagon in the spiral. The colour of the triangles goes from black, to grey, to white. The two short lines alternate between thick and thin.

Checkpoint 1

Page 24

1 E:

All the other images contain two identical shapes.

2 A:

The arrow turns clockwise in all the other images.

3 C:

In all the other images, the white shape has an even number of sides and the black shape has an odd number of sides.

4 B:

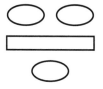

The images on the left all contain a horizontal rectangle with more shapes above it than below it.

5 D:

All the images on the left have thick horizontal stripes.

6 E:

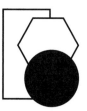

The black shape is at the front in all of the other images.

Page 25

7 C:

The arrow moves anticlockwise around the square. The dotted and solid lines form two squares stood on a vertex.

8 A:

A continuous path runs across the squares. A is the only option that doesn't break it.

9 A:

Reading clockwise around the grid, each arrow points to the next triangle. The small triangles alternate between black and white.

10 B:

Reading clockwise in a spiral from the top left hexagon, each hexagon adds one line.

5 Codes in boxes

Page 26 Guided questions

1 A:

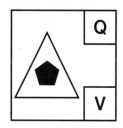

The top letter shows the inner shape (Q – pentagon, K – circle). The bottom letter shows the colour of the inner shape (R – white, V – black).

2 E:

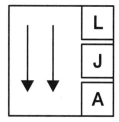

The top letter shows the position of the lines (X – crossed, L – parallel). The middle letter shows the thickness of the lines (D – thick, J – thin). The bottom letter shows the position of the arrowheads (A – on different lines, B – on the same line).

Page 27 Guided questions

1 D:

The top letter shows the number of points on the star (M – five, Y – six, G – seven). The middle letter shows whether a rectangle is present (P – rectangle, Q – no rectangle). The bottom letter shows the pattern (T – dots, U – stripes).

2 C:

The top letter shows the number of areas the shape is divided into (Z – two, Y – four). The middle letter shows the fill pattern (M – black, I – dotted). The bottom letter shows the outer shape (O – point going out, U – point going in).

Page 27 Have a go

1 A:

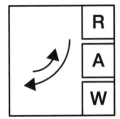

The top letter shows whether the short line has an arrow head (R – arrowhead, O – no arrowhead). The middle letter shows the thickness of the lines (S – thick, A – thin). The bottom letter shows whether the long line has an arrowhead (W – arrowhead, G – no arrowhead).

2 B:

The top letter shows the colour of the inner shape (H – grey, U – patterned). The middle letter shows whether the two shapes are the same (D – same, B – different). The bottom letter shows the angle of pattern (E – diagonal lines, T – vertical and horizontal lines).

Page 28 Have a go

1 A:

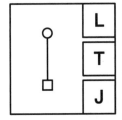

The top letter shows the top shape (I – square, L – circle). The middle letter shows the colour of the top shape (T – white, Y – black). The bottom letter shows whether the two shapes are the same (R – same, J – different).

2 D:

The top letter shows the black shape (R – square, S – circle). The middle letter shows the size of the black shape (O – large, Z – small). The bottom letter shows the position of the black shape (X – middle, F – bottom).

3 E:

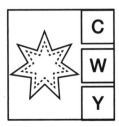

The top letter shows the number of points the stars have (N – six, C – seven). The middle letter shows the line style of the inner star (V – solid, W – dashed). The bottom letter shows the line style of the outer star (Y – solid, Z – dashed).

4 C:

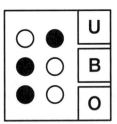

The top letter shows the position of the black spot in the top row (P – left, U – right). The middle letter shows the position of the black spot in the middle row (B – left, M – right). The bottom letter shows the position of the black spot in the bottom row (O – left, F – right).

Page 29 Timed practice

1 B:

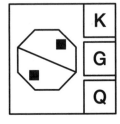

The top letter shows the number of lines in the shape (K – one, B – two). The middle letter shows the colour of the squares (G – black, H – white). The bottom letter shows the number of squares (Q – two, R – three).

2 E:

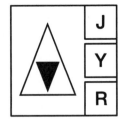

The top letter shows the orientation of the inner triangle (V – point up, J – point down). The middle letter shows the orientation of the outer triangle (Y – point up, O – point down). The bottom letter shows the colour of the triangles (D – white inner, black outer, R – black inner, white outer).

3 C: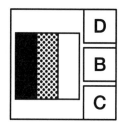

The top letter shows the position of the black rectangle (D – left, O – middle). The middle letter shows the position of the white rectangle (E – left, B – right, L – middle). The bottom letter shows the position of the dotted rectangle (K – right, F – left, C – middle).

4 E: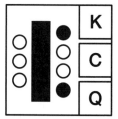

The top letter shows the thickness of the line (S – thin, K – thick). The middle letter shows which side has the most circles (N – left, C – right). The bottom letter shows the number of black circles (F – one, Q – two).

5 A: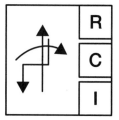

The top letter shows if the straight line is an arrow (R – arrow, U – line). The middle letter shows whether the curved line has an arrowhead (C – arrowhead, A – no arrowhead). The bottom letter shows whether the angled line has an arrowhead (I – arrow, E – line).

6 Codes in lists

Page 30 Guided questions

1 B:

IW

The first letter shows the position of the oval (I – left, P – right). The second letter shows whether the arrow is pointing into or out of the oval (S – in, W – out).

2 A:

DZL

The first letter shows the number of arrowheads (W – none, D – one, C – two). The second letter shows the path of the curve (V – down to the left, X – down to the right, Z – up to the left). The third letter shows the thickness of the line (P – thin, L – thick).

Page 31 Guided questions

1 C:

AMJ

The first letter shows the number of triangles (A – two, F – three). The second letter shows the type of the triangles (M – equilateral, L – isosceles). The third letter shows the orientation of the triangles (J – point up, K – point to the right).

2 B:

FVN

The first letter shows the angle of the stripes (U – horizontal, F – vertical, S – diagonal). The second letter shows the colour of the square (T – grey, X – white, V – black). The third letter shows the presence or absence of a white circle (O – white circle, N – no white circle).

Page 31 Have a go

1 D:

IOT

The first letter shows the orientation of the star (J – two points at the top and bottom, I – two points at the side). The second letter shows the presence of a circle (D – circle present, O – no circle). The third letter shows the presence of a square (T – square present, F – no square).

2 C:

TYG

The first letter shows the type of shape in the middle (L – hexagon, T – rectangle, I – circle). The second letter shows the type of shape on the right (K – triangle, N – circle, Y – hexagon). The third letter shows the position of the black square (G – left, Z – middle, H – right).

Page 32 Have a go

1 C: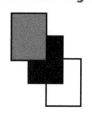

YQW

The first letter shows the order of the rectangles (Z – top rectangle behind, Y – top rectangle in front). The second letter shows the position of the black rectangle (T – at the bottom, Q – in the middle). The third letter shows the position of the grey rectangle (C – at the bottom, I – in the middle, W – at the top).

2 E:

The first letter shows the number of points the star has (G – five, T – six, R – seven). The second letter shows the colour of the triangle (M – black, N – white, W – grey). The third letter shows the orientation of the triangle (P – point up, D – point down).

3 E:

The first letter shows the direction of the arrows (U – pointing in the same direction, L – pointing in different directions). The second letter shows the colour of the circle (Y – black, F – white). The third letter shows the position of the shapes (V – circle below the curve, D – circle above the curve).

4 D:

The first letter shows which column the filled square is in (A – left, B – middle, C – right). The second letter shows which row the filled square is in (X – top, Y – middle, Z – bottom). The third letter shows the direction of the diagonal line (G – top left to bottom right, H – top right to bottom left).

Page 33 Timed practice

1 B:

The first letter shows the thickness of the spiral line (M – thick, Q – thin). The second letter shows the orientation of the spiral (U – ends at the bottom, R – ends at the top).

2 B:

The first letter shows the pattern on the oval (D – dotted, T – white). The second letter shows whether the oval and the outer rectangle have the same shading (O – same, A – different). The third letter shows the shading of the inner rectangle (G – crosshatch, N – dotted, B – white).

3 E:

The first letter shows the orientation of the straight lines (H – bottom, E – top). The second letter shows the number of black rings (W – one ring, Y – two rings, L – three rings). The third letter shows the colour of the outer ring (M – black, O – white).

4 C:

The first letter shows the thickness of the outside line (G – thick, J – thin). The second letter shows the pattern of the inner circle (N – dotted, A – stripes). The third letter shows the size of the section removed from the inner circle (V – large, C – small).

5 B:

The first letter shows the number of points the top left star has (C – five, B – six, A – seven). The second letter shows the number of points the top right star has (D – five, F – six, E – seven). The third letter shows the number of points the bottom star has (H – five, G – six, I – seven).

Checkpoint 2

Page 34

1 B: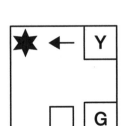

The top letter shows the position of the small square (G – top, J – bottom). The bottom letter shows the colour of the small square (V – black, Z – white).

2 E: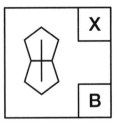

The top letter shows which shape the arrow is pointing at (L – square, Y – star). The bottom letter shows the black shape (R – square, G – star).

3 D: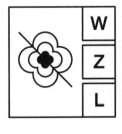

The top letter shows whether there is an arrowhead at the top (R – arrowhead, X – no arrowhead). The bottom letter shows whether there is an arrowhead at the bottom (G – arrowhead, B – no arrowhead).

4 E:

The top letter shows the outer colour (W – white, F – black). The middle letter shows the middle colour (Z – white, T – black). The bottom letter shows the centre colour (P – white, L – black).

5 A:

The top letter shows the orientation of the top triangles (S – two pointing up, O – two pointing down). The middle letter shows the orientation of the middle triangles (M – two pointing up, N – two pointing down). The bottom letter shows the orientation of the bottom triangles (P – two pointing up, A – two pointing down).

Page 35

6 E:

DU

The first letter shows the direction of the diagonal line (D – top right to bottom left, E – top left to bottom right). The second letter shows the orientation of the rounded square (U – side at the top and bottom, Y – vertex at the top and bottom).

7 A:

CK

The first letter shows the colour of the innermost star (R – grey, C – black). The second letter shows the colour of the outermost star (P – white, Z – black, K – grey).

8 B:

XBZ

The first letter shows the line style of the rectangle (A – dashed, X – solid). The second letter shows whether the line is inside or outside the star (Y – inside, B – outside). The third letter shows the number of points the star has (C – five, Z – six).

9 C:

ZS

The first letter shows the orientation of the heptagon (B – vertex at the bottom, Z – side at the bottom). The second letter shows the relative position of the two lines (C – meet at a point, P – cross over, S – parallel).

10 E:

DAN

The first letter shows the top left shape (D – square, T – triangle). The second letter shows the top right shape (I – circle, O – triangle, A – square). The third letter shows the bottom shape (P – triangle, E – square, N – circle).

7 Which cube does not match the net?

Page 36 Guided questions

1 A:

The triangle and the crossed arrows point towards each other on the net.

2 B:

On the net, the bold arrow points at the dotted square.

Page 37 Guided questions

1 E:

The net shows that the T shape and the white and grey square should be on opposite faces.

2 B:

The star is upside down.

Page 37 Have a go

1 D:

There is no triangle on the net.

2 A:

The arrow points at the white T on the net.

Page 38 Have a go

1 D:

The thick black arrow points at the black circle on the net.

2 C:

The black hexagons should be in the top left and the bottom right of the grid.

3 C:

The hatched circle is next to the white half of the circle on the net.

4 C:

The double-headed arrow points to the corner between the triangle and the striped square on the net.

Page 39 Timed practice

1 A:

There is no white triangle on the net.

2 C:

The black rectangle's short edge touches the hatched pattern on the net.

3 E:

On the net, the black L shape does not touch the face with the circle.

4 D:

One of the two dots is in the corner next to the white square on the net.

5 E:

The faces with the two squares and the crossed circle are the other way around on the net.

8 Which net matches the cube?

Page 40 Guided questions

1 A:

In B, the dotted side only has two dots. In C, the top of the T will not be next to the dotted side. D will not make a cube.

2 D: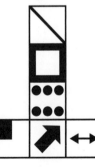

In A, the small black square would not touch the dotted face. In B, the large arrow is white, not black. C would not make a cube.

Page 41 Guided questions

1 B: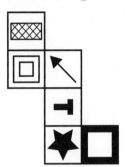

In C and D, the arrow is pointing away from the square. In A, the arrow starts at the bottom of the T.

2 B: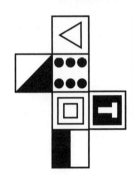

In A and C, the short ends of the black and white rectangles should be next to the squares. In D, the face with two squares is missing the small square.

Page 41 Have a go

1 A: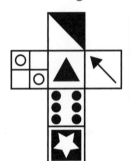

In B, the face with the white dots is rotated incorrectly. C has four black dots instead of six. D would not make a cube.

2 D: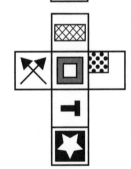

In A and C, the square with black dots should be next to the grey square. In B and C, the long side of the hatched rectangle should be next to the grey square.

Page 42 Have a go

1 B:

In A, the white triangle should be next to the black cross. In C, the face with the black squares is orientated incorrectly. In D, the black cross is too thick.

2 C: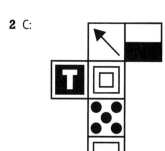

In A and D, the bottom of the white T should be next to the dots. In B, the white T and the single square are the wrong way around.

4 D: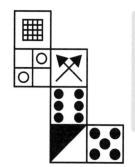

In A, the five dots are on the wrong side. In B, the black and white triangle and the five dots are opposite each other. In C, the white triangle should be next to the five dots.

3 C: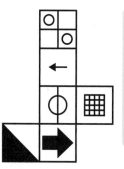

In A, the thick black arrow is facing the wrong way. In B, the three arrows, circles and triangles will not line up correctly. In D, the line through the circle should be at a right angle to the thick arrow.

5 B:

In A, C and D, the dotted square is not touching the crossed circle and the four dots.

4 A: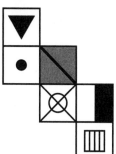

In B, the crossed circle and dot are the wrong way around. In C, the striped square is the wrong way around. In D, the dot and the striped square are the wrong way around.

9 Non-cube nets

Page 44 Guided question

1 A: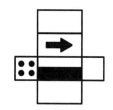

In B and D, the arrow is pointing towards the four dots. In C, the black side of the black and white rectangle is next to the arrow.

Page 43 Timed practice

1 B: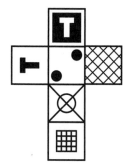

A is missing the white T. C is missing the black T. In D, the black T face should be one square above.

Page 45 Guided questions

1 B:

C would not make a hexagonal prism. In A, the top point of the star is not next to the patterned hexagon. In D, there is a gap between the patterned squares.

2 B:

In A, the black triangle should be to the left of the striped face. The diagonal stripes in C are going in the wrong direction. In D, the black triangle and the striped faces are opposite each other.

2 A: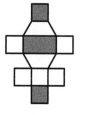

B does not have a grey rectangle. C does not make the 3D solid. In D, the grey square is in the wrong position.

3 D: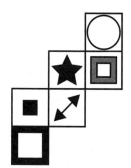

In A and C, the double-ended arrow is pointing to the wrong corner. In B, the square and the arrow are opposite each other.

3 D:

In B, the white isosceles triangle is not in between the other two isosceles triangles. In A and C, the crosshatched face and the dotted face are the wrong way around.

Page 46 Have a go

1 C: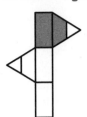

In A, the middle rectangle should be grey and the bottom rectangle should be white. In B, the top rectangle should be grey. D does not have a small white triangle.

2 B:

In A, the stripes on the square should be diagonal. In C, the black and white segments on the triangle are the wrong way around. D does not make the 3D solid.

3 A:

A is the only net that has alternating grey and white triangles.

Page 47 Timed practice

1 A:

In B and C, the top of the T shape should be next to the face with the black triangle. In D, the grey square should be white.

2 C:

A and D both have an isosceles triangle with its point next to the small triangles. This means they would not make the 3D solid. In B, the two patterned isosceles triangles would not be next to each other.

3 C: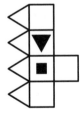

A and B will not make the 3D solid. In D, the triangle and the square should be the other way around.

4 A:

In B, the two outer triangles would overlap. In C, the three outer triangles would overlap. In D, the outer triangle is grey.

Checkpoint 3

Page 48

1 E:

The circle does not appear on the net.

2 A:

The base of the T is next to the black and white circle on the net.

3 B:

The point of the triangle is next to the thick cross on the net.

4 C:

The arrow points to the grid on the net.

5 D: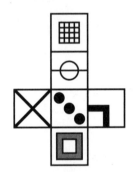

In A, part of the black L shape should point to the dots. In B, there are only two dots. In C, the colours of the grey and white squares have swapped.

6 A: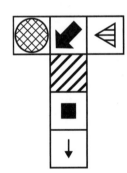

In B and C, the small arrow should point away from the black square. In D, the striped triangle should point in the same direction as the small arrow.

Page 49

7 C: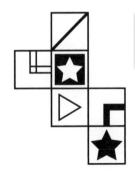

In A, B and D, the black L shape is touching the white star face.

8 B: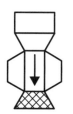

In A, C and D, the arrow does not point at the crosshatched trapezium.

9 B:

A will not make a 3D solid. In C and D, the patterned triangle and the patterned trapezium are not touching.

10 C:

C is the only net where two grey trapeziums touch along their long edges.

10 2D views of 3D solids

Page 50 Guided questions

1 A:

The correct answer must have one square in the left column, three squares in the middle column and two squares in the right column. Only A matches this description.

2 E:

The correct answer must have three squares in the left and right columns and one square at the bottom in the middle two columns. Only E matches this description.

Page 51 Guided questions

1 D: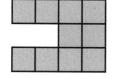

The correct answer must have two squares on the left in the bottom row, two squares on the right in the middle row and three squares in the top row. Only D matches this description.

2 E:

The correct answer must have one square at the bottom in the left column and three squares in the middle and right columns. Only E matches this description.

3 B:

The correct answer must have two squares in the left two columns (one at the top and one at the bottom) and three squares in the right two columns. Only B matches this description.

Page 51 Have a go

1 E:

The correct answer must have three squares on the bottom row, two squares in the right in the middle row and one square in the middle on the top row. Only E matches this description.

Page 52 Have a go

1 A: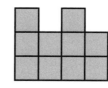

The correct answer must have three squares in the first and third columns, and two squares at the bottom in the second and fourth columns. Only A matches this description.

2 D: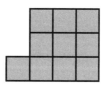

The correct answer must have one square at the bottom in the left column and three squares in the other three columns. Only D matches this description.

3 B: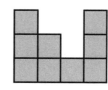

The correct answer must have three squares in the first column, two squares in the second column, one square in the third column and three squares in the fourth column. Only B matches this description.

4 E: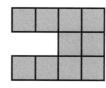

The correct answer must have two squares in the left two columns (one at the top and one at the bottom) and three squares in the right two columns. Only E matches this description.

Page 53 Timed practice

1 C:

The correct answer must have two squares in the bottom and middle rows, and one square on the left in the top row. Only C matches this description.

2 A:

The correct answer must have three squares in the left column, two squares at the top in the middle column and two squares in the right column (one at the top and one at the bottom). Only A matches this description.

3 C:

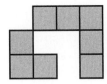

The correct answer must have two squares at the bottom in the first column, two squares in the second column (one at the top and one at the bottom), one square at the top in the third column and three squares in the fourth column. Only C matches this description.

4 B:

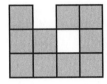

The correct answer must have three squares in the first column, two squares at the bottom in the second column, two squares in the third column (one at the top and one at the bottom) and three squares in the fourth column. Only B matches this description.

5 E:

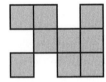

The correct answer must have two squares in the first column (one at the top and one at the bottom), two squares at the top in the second column, two squares at the bottom in the third column and three squares in the fourth column. Only E matches this description.

11 3D rotation

Page 55 Guided questions

1 C:

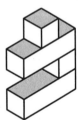

The solid in the view is made from two cubes and two parallel cuboids. C is the only option made of these shapes.

2 E:

E is the only solid where one cuboid touches all three other shapes. In the view in the question, it has been turned upside down.

3 B:

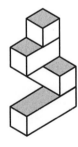

The solid in the view has one cube and three cuboids, so C and D are wrong. It also has four shapes in a row, so A and E are wrong. The answer must be B.

4 E:

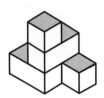

The solid in the view does not contain a T shape, so D is wrong. It has one cube on a small cuboid, so A and C are wrong. The cuboids in B would go the wrong way, so the answer must be E.

Page 56 Have a go

1 A:

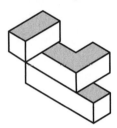

B, D and E do not have L shapes, so must be wrong. C is made of four shapes, so the answer must be A.

2 C:

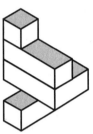

The solid in the view has four shapes in a row. C is the only option with four shapes in a row.

3 E:

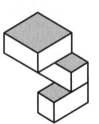

E is the only option that contains a long cuboid between two other shapes, so it must be the answer.

4 C:

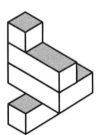

The solid in the view contains two cuboids of the same length. C is the only option that contains these, so it must be right.

Page 57 Timed practice

1 C:

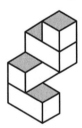

The solid in the view is made from four shapes. C is the only option made from four shapes.

2 E:

The solid contains a T shape, which rules out A, C and D. The central shape in the view is a cuboid. The central shape in B is a cube, so E must be the answer.

3 D:

The solid in the view contains an L shape and a long cuboid. D is the only option that has these shapes.

4 A:

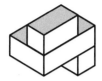

The solid in the view contains a cube, an L shape and a short cuboid. A is the only option that has these shapes.

5 E:

The solid has a T shape, which rules out options A, C and D. The shape joined to the T is a cuboid, so E must be the answer.

12 Different views of 3D solids

Page 58 Guided questions

1 D:

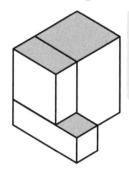

In A, the bottom cuboid is split into two shapes. In B and C, the top cuboid at the front is split into two shapes.

2 C:

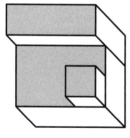

In A, the cube on top of the solid is on the left. In B, the cuboid at the back of the solid is too tall, so you can see too much of the white side. In D, the cuboid at the back is too short and is in line with the shape in front.

Page 59 Guided question

1 B:

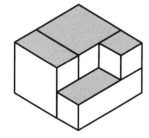

In A, the large cube has been split into two shapes. In C, the large cube is in the wrong place. In D, the large cube and the cuboid at the back have been merged into one shape.

Page 59 Have a go

1 B:

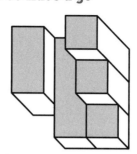

In C, the cuboids on the right do not step down in height. In A, the left cuboid is too small. In D it is too tall.

2 A:

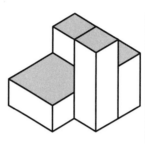

B has been rotated too far – the tall cuboid on the right of the original 3D solid should be at the front. In C, the bottom cuboid is too small. In D, the tall cuboid has been split into two shapes.

Page 60 Have a go

1 D:

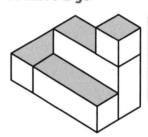

The small cube at the top of the solid is missing in A and B. The near-left cuboid is missing in C.

2 A:

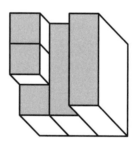

Three of the shapes are the same height in the 3D solid. This isn't the case in B, C and D.

3 B:

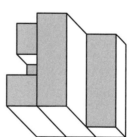

C has three shapes the same height. A has a gap in the bottom left layer. In D, the cube on the left side is too short.

Page 61 Timed practice

1 C:

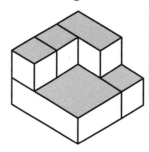

A and B do not have shapes in an L pattern on the top. In D, the bottom cuboid is split into two shapes.

2 C:

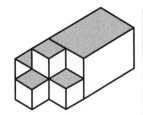

In A, there is an extra shape visible at the back. In B, the left cube on the original 3D solid is missing. In D, the cube on the top layer is in the wrong position.

3 A:

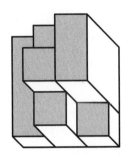

In B, the cuboid on the right is too small. In C, the back centre cuboid is too small. In D, it is too tall.

4 B:

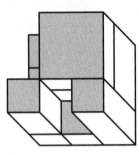

When viewed from the top, the 3D solid should have one large square and two small squares, all of the same height. B is the only option with the shapes at the correct height.

13 Build the 3D solid

Page 62 Guided questions

1 B:

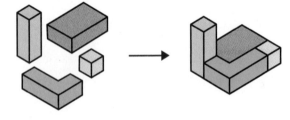

2 D:

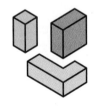

Page 63 Guided question

1 B:

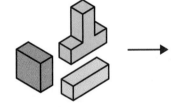

Page 63 Have a go

1 B:

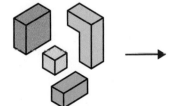 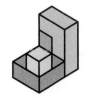

2 A:

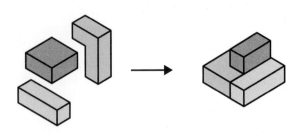

Page 64 Have a go

1 D:

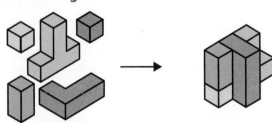

The purple cube is hidden behind the other blocks.

2 C:

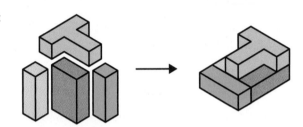

3 A:

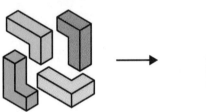 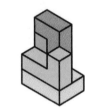

Page 65 Timed practice

1 B:

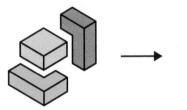

2 C:

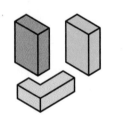 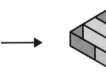

3 D:

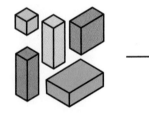 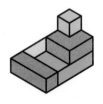

4 B:

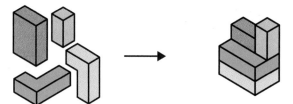

14 Fold and punch

Page 66 Guided questions

1 D:

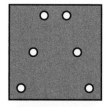

A has not been reflected. In B, the line of symmetry is not in the middle of the paper. C is missing the three holes on the left.

2 D:

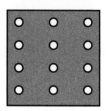

A and B are missing one row of holes. C is missing two rows of holes.

Page 67 Guided questions

1 C:

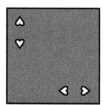

A and D have the wrong number of holes. In B, the hearts have not been reflected.

2 D:

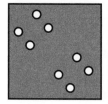

In A, there are not enough holes – this is what it would look like if the paper had only been folded once from corner to corner. In B, only the bottom four holes are present. In C, there are only three holes on each side.

3 B:

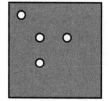

A has too many holes on the part that wasn't folded. C is missing the holes from the part that wasn't folded. In D, the top hole is in the wrong place.

Page 67 Have a go

1 C:

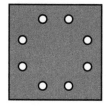

A is missing holes at the top and bottom. B is missing holes at the bottom and on the left. D is missing two holes at the bottom. Only C has the correct number of holes.

Page 68 Have a go

1 B:

Only the first fold affects the holes. A and C have too many holes on the left. In D, the bottom hole should be pointing right, not down.

2 B:

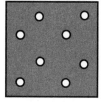

In A, there are no holes in the top right of the paper. In C, the paper hasn't been folded the second time, so the top right and bottom left holes are missing. In D, the holes are the wrong shape and the top right hole is missing.

3 A:

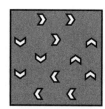

In B and C, there are the wrong number of holes and the holes are the wrong shape. In D, the holes are pointing the wrong way.

4 C:

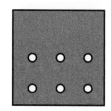

In A, the two left holes are missing. In B, there are an extra three holes at the top. In D, three of the holes are missing.

Page 69 Timed practice

1 B:

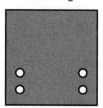

A and D are missing two holes. In C, only the bottom half of the page has been folded, so the top holes are too high up.

2 A:

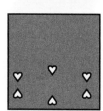

C and D are missing three holes. In B, the hearts have not been reflected.

3 D:

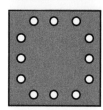

A, B and C are all missing holes. Only D has the correct number of holes.

4 B:

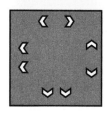

A has the wrong shaped holes. In C, the holes are in the wrong place. D is missing the top left holes.

5 A: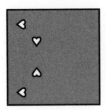

In B, the top left and bottom left hearts have not been reflected properly. The right side of the paper was folded less than halfway and had no holes punched in it, so the holes on the right side of B, C and D are wrong.

Progress test

Page 70

1 E:

All of the other images have a grey half.

2 A:

In all of the other images, the bottom horizontal shape is behind the vertical shape.

3 B:

The images on the left have three lines going from point to point across the stars. One of the lines joins opposite points.

4 B:

The images on the left contain two identical regular polygons rotated so that their vertices are evenly spaced. There is a smaller version of the same shape in the middle.

5 D:

Reading clockwise around the grid, the shape rotates 90° in each square.

Page 71

6 C:

The diagonals running from top-left to bottom-right have the same shape. The diagonals running from top-right to bottom-left have the same pattern.

7 A:

The smallest triangles alternate between black and white. The middle and largest triangles swap patterns with those opposite them.

8 C:

Reading in a spiral up and clockwise from the centre, a circle is added in each hexagon. The circles alternate between black and white at each step.

9 D: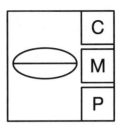

The first letter shows the width of the shape (C – wide, J – narrow). The second letter shows the orientation of the line in the middle (R – vertical, M – horizontal). The third letter shows the height of the shape (O – tall, P – short).

10 D: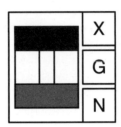

The first letter shows the orientation of the largest rectangles (X – standing on long side, Y – standing on short side). The second letter shows the orientation of the black, white and grey stripe (R – horizontal, G – vertical). The third letter shows the order of the black and grey rectangles (H – black on the left, P – black on the right, N – black on the top).

Page 72

11 A:

AJW

The first letter shows the number of points the star has (F – seven, A – eight, C – nine). The second letter shows the number of lines inside the star (J – one, B – two, P – three). The third letter shows the colour of the star (T – grey, W – white).

12 B:

IHN

The first letter shows the colour of the innermost ring (L – black, I – white). The second letter shows the colour of the outermost ring (H – black, Q – white). The third letter shows the colour of the ring inside that (N – black, D – white).

13 B:

The bold arrow should point to the chequered face.

14 C:

The face with two dots should be next to the white rectangle.

15 A:

The triangle is rotated incorrectly in B, C and D. In B and D, the diagonal stripes are also going the wrong way.

Page 73

16 D: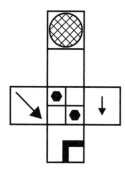

In A, the two small hexagons are in the wrong squares. In B, the black L should be in the top left corner. In C, the large arrow should point to the top right corner.

17 B:

In A and D, the small white triangle and the grey trapezium should be the opposite colours. C would not make the 3D solid.

18 C: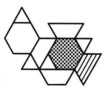

In A, B and D, the short side of the trapezium is not next to the dotted hexagon. D would not make the 3D solid.

19 B:

The correct answer must have two cubes in the bottom row on the left, two cubes in the middle row on the right and three cubes in the top row.

20 D: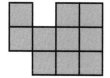

The correct answer must have two cubes at the top in the first column, two cubes at the bottom in the second column and three cubes in the third and fourth columns.

Page 74

21 E: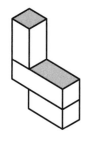

B and D are both too wide to make the rotated solid. In A, the bottom cuboid should not align with the other two on the right. In C, the top cuboid should be on the right.

22 B: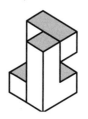

A, C and E are not wide enough to make the rotated solid. The shape at the back of the 3D solid has to be an L shape, which D does not have, so B must be the answer.

23 B: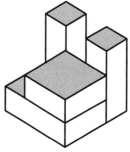

There are two cuboids at the back left of the 3D solid that are taller than the other shapes. In A, C and D, at least one of these cuboids is too short.

24 B: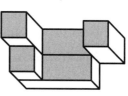

In A and C, the cube has been merged into another shape. In D, the cuboid at the back is too tall.

Page 75

25 C: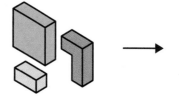

26 B: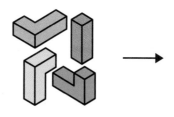

The short end of the yellow L shape is hidden behind the green shape.

27 C: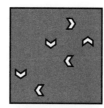

A and B do not have enough holes to be the correct answer. In D, the top right two arrows are pointing in the wrong direction.

28 A: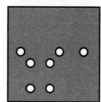

The paper should have seven holes in total. B, C and D all have the wrong number of holes.

Puzzle maker

Use the templates to create your own questions.

Complete the square grid

Section 3

Complete the hexagonal grid

Section 4

Codes in boxes

Section 5

Which cube does not match the net?

Section 7

Use one of the nets on the next page to help you.

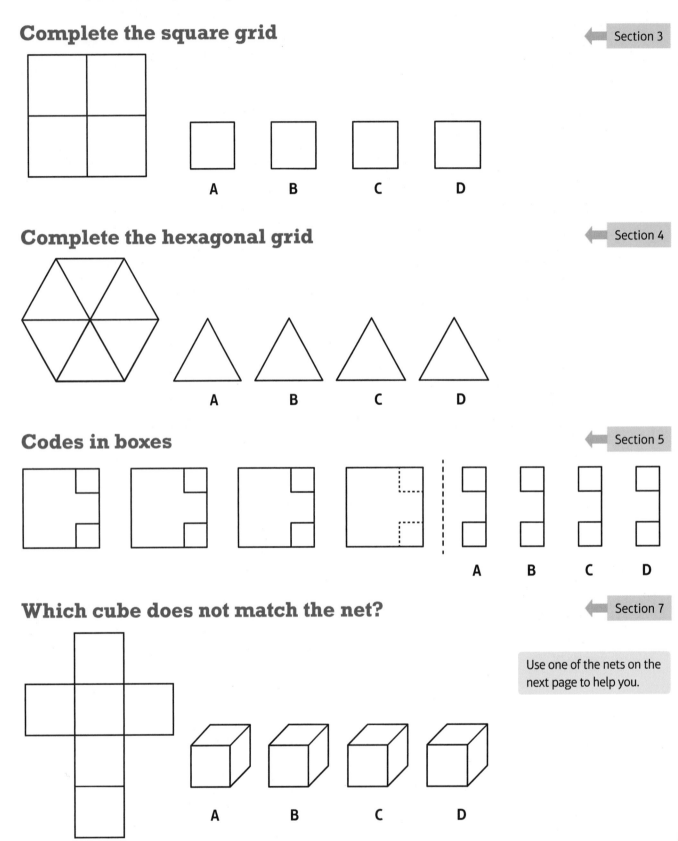

Cube nets

These pages show you all 11 ways to draw a cube net. Trace the nets and cut them out to see how they work. Draw patterns on them and fold them up to check your answers to the questions with cubes and nets in practice sections 7 and 8.

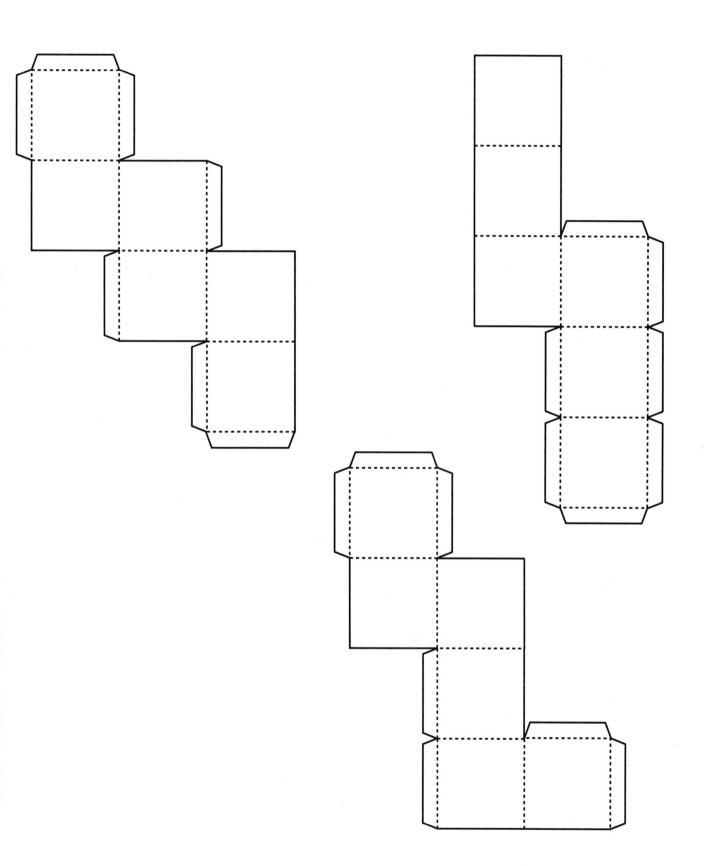

Notes

Progress chart

Use this chart to keep track of your 11+ journey. Fill in your marks as you complete each *Timed practice* section and check off any extra practice you do.

	Timed practice	Digital questions	Ten-minute test
Diagnostic test	/28		
1 Odd one out	/5	✓	✓
2 Which image belongs?	/5	✓	✓
3 Complete the square grid	/4	✓	✓
4 Complete the hexagonal grid	/4	✓	✓
Checkpoint 1	/10	✓	
5 Codes in boxes	/5	✓	✓
6 Codes in lists	/5	✓	✓
Checkpoint 2	/10	✓	
7 Which cube does not match the net?	/5	✓	✓
8 Which net matches the cube?	/5	✓	✓
9 Non-cube nets	/4	✓	✓
Checkpoint 3	/10	✓	
10 2D views of 3D solids	/5	✓	✓
11 3D rotation	/5	✓	✓
12 Different views of 3D solids	/4	✓	✓
13 Build the 3D solid	/4	✓	✓
14 Fold and punch	/5	✓	✓
Progress test	/28	✓	

Published by Pearson Education Limited, 80 Strand, London, WC2R 0RL.

www.pearsonschools.co.uk

Text © Pearson Education Limited 2018
Edited, typeset and produced by Elektra Media Ltd
Original illustrations © Pearson Education Limited 2018
Cover illustration by Lukas Bischoff

The right of Gareth Moore to be identified as author of this work has been asserted by him in accordance with the Copyright, Designs and Patents Act 1988.

First published 2018

21 20 19 18
10 9 8 7 6 5 4 3 2 1

British Library Cataloguing in Publication Data
A catalogue record for this book is available from the British Library

ISBN: 978 1 292 24657 4

Printed in Italy by L.E.G.O. S.p.A.